TAROT
at a Crossroads

"This book is destined to become a Tarot classic. It fills a unique spot in the literature, bridging the gap between traditional divinatory Tarot readers and psychotherapists/counselors wishing to weave this powerful tool into their own practices. I'm especially impressed by the generosity of the authors in their open-handed instructions on the use of techniques they have personally pioneered. There is much here to enlighten not only the beginner but also those who've used Tarot for years."

—**David Van Nuys, PhD**
Emeritus Professor of Psychology

"A very informative, thought-provoking and useful crossover between psychology and Tarot. A lot to think about and absorb. What is obvious and standard for one side of the psychologist-Tarot reader equation will be useful and original to the other. You will be a better Tarot card reader or a better psychotherapist or counselor after you have read this book. It will take you places you have not been before."

—**Wald Amberstone**
Director, The Tarot School and Reader's Studio Conference

"[This] book is fun, creative, deep, and full of usable information and ways to immediately engage with the cards to enhance self-knowledge. It is written in a way that allows both psychotherapists and Tarot readers to use its information and exercises with equal ease. With great pleasure and anticipation, I invite you now to open this book and look inside at yourself."

—**Elinor Greenberg, PhD, GGP**
Co-chair of New York Institute of Gestalt Therapy Program Committee

DEDICATION

Our heartfelt love and infinite thanks to
Helen, the Queen of Swords,
Martha Marie, The Queen of Cups,
and Mata Amritanandamayi, The High Priestess.

TAROT
at a *Crossroads*

THE UNEXPECTED MEETING
OF TAROT & PSYCHOLOGY

Kooch N. Daniels, MA, and Victor Daniels, PhD

Schiffer Publishing Ltd®

4880 Lower Valley Road • Atglen, PA 19310

Please note that the material within this book is not intended to be used as treatment for any form of psychological or physical disorder. The authors or publisher make no claims or take any responsibility for healing problems. When using the information provided in relation to the Tarot cards, the authors advise novice readers, Tarot professionals, and licensed practitioners of counseling or psychotherapy to work within the framework of their expertise.

Cover design by Justin Watkinson
Type set in Minion

ISBN: 978-0-7643-5186-0
Printed in China

Published by Schiffer Publishing, Ltd.
4880 Lower Valley Road
Atglen, PA 19310
Phone: (610) 593-1777; Fax: (610) 593-2002
E-mail: Info@schifferbooks.com
Web: www.schifferbooks.com

For our complete selection of fine books on this and related subjects, please visit our website at www.schifferbooks.com. You may also write for a free catalog.

Schiffer Publishing's titles are available at special discounts for bulk purchases for sales promotions or premiums. Special editions, including personalized covers, corporate imprints, and excerpts, can be created in large quantities for special needs. For more information, contact the publisher.

We are always looking for people to write books on new and related subjects. If you have an idea for a book, please contact us at proposals@schifferbooks.com.

CONTENTS

ACKNOWLEDGMENTS

We are most grateful to Wald Amberstone, impresario of the annual New York Reader's Studio Tarot conference and the accompanying Psychology and Tarot Conference. One day at lunch during the 2013 conference we were discussing the approach we had developed for using the Tarot in psychotherapy and counseling, as well as what psychology had to offer Tarot readers, when he suddenly said, "Why don't you write a book about it?" Because Kooch already had an outline for a Tarot and psychology e-book, she was delighted with Wald's encouragement. Also, we'd like to thank his wife, Ruth Ann, a bright star in the Tarot community who with Wald invited us to address their Psychology and Tarot Conference in 2014. An oasis of Tarot and psychology enthusiasm, it brings people together to blend these two sometimes contrary approaches to studying the human mind and potential. We can't offer enough gratitude to the many people we met there who became our friends and sources of inspiration.

Wald Amberstone also was kind enough to be one of our prepublication readers of our manuscript. We thank him along with David Van Nuys, PhD, Host of *Shrink Rap Radio*, and Lila Welchel, MEd, for taking the time to read, give insightful suggestions, and encourage our writing.

We also owe a special debt of gratitude to Therese Thalassa Porter, originator of the annual BATS, the Bay Area Tarot Symposium in Northern California. For over two decades she has blessed our local Tarot community by bringing many of the brightest and most influential thinkers in the Tarot world together under one roof. There we met a long list of contemporary Tarot scholars, authors, deck creators, and enthusiasts who encouraged us to think about our work in new ways. At BATS we were also fortunate to meet Chris McClure, marketing representative at Schiffer Publishing, and we want to especially thank him for encouraging us to send Schiffer our book proposal.

We are equally grateful to the peer review and program committees of the "Association for the Advancement of Gestalt Therapy—An International Community" for their open minded invitations to present at their 2005 Amsterdam conference where we first started teaching "The Use of Tarot In Therapy," and later at the 2012 biannual conference in Puebla, Mexico, and the 2014 conference in Asilomar, California, where we offered workshops based on a more fully developed model of our working process. Also, we'd like to thank the Mexican Gestalt Association for inviting us to present our therapeutic approach at its very first annual conference in Guadalajara in 2013.

We are also grateful to trailblazer and pivotal thinker Art Rosengarten for his expansive influence in the twin worlds of psychotherapy and the Tarot. We owe gratitude to the many key speakers who appeared on the *Tarot Blog Talk Radio* show *Kosmic Koffee With Kooch*. We give a special round of applause to Elinor Greenburg, Mary Greer, Katrina Wynne, Thomas Caldwell, James Wells, and Jenne Perlstein, who spoke on the merits of psychology and Tarot. And Kooch especially wants to thank Dax Carlisle, founder of the Tarot Guild and host of her show for giving her the opportunity to interview so many amazing people in the Tarot and New Age community.

Our book would be words without pictures if not for the generosity of the Tarot artists and deck creators who have given us permission to use their beautiful cards. Words are not enough to thank Jude Simmons, Robert Place, Major Tom Schick, Anna Franklin, Yoav Ben-Dov, Marie White, Courtney Weber, Beth Seilonen, George Courtney, Aunia Kahn and Russell Moon, Jasmine Beckett-Griffith and J.R. Rivera, and European card publisher A.G.M-Urania for their generosity.

We especially appreciate the insightful guidance of our editor, Dinah Roseberry at Schiffer Publishing.

If we have not named you here, but you nonetheless know that you've touched us deeply by working alongside us, coming to our classes, doing readings for us, or letting us do readings or Tarot-enhanced gestalt therapy sessions for you, we graciously and gratefully thank you, too. Also, we are deeply grateful to our daughters, Tara and Lila, and our extended family and friends because our life would be empty without you. We also want to give thanks to our amazing teachers, mystic scholar Harish Johari, and India's Hugging Saint, Mata Amritanandamayi. Also, with a humble bow, we give thanks to the Divine Presence in life who offers the opportunity to walk, skip, or run the sacred, zigzagging path of "The Fool's journey."

FOREWORD

I became a Gestalt therapist because I like the "Aha!" experience, the sudden and unexpected insights that Gestalt awareness experiments can bring. I took up Tarot because I felt a mysterious pull to explore the meaning of the exotic images on the cards and understand how they might relate to me and my clients. Eventually, I joined my two worlds together, psychotherapy and Tarot, and I went looking for kindred spirits who had done the same.

I found them at a Gestalt therapy conference in Mexico in a presentation by Kooch and Victor Daniels. Now they have written the book that I wished I could have read when I first started my Gestalt therapy and Tarot journey. Like Kooch and Victor themselves, their book is fun, creative, deep, and full of usable information and ways to immediately engage with the cards to enhance self-knowledge. It is written in a way that allows both psychotherapists and Tarot readers to use its information and exercises with equal ease. With great pleasure and anticipation, I invite you now to open this book and look inside at yourself.

—Elinor Greenberg, PhD, CGP
Co-Chair of Program Committee at the New York Institute for Gestalt Therapy

ARTISTS AND ILLUSTRATIONS

We are deeply indebted to the artists and publishers who generously allowed us to use cards from their decks to illustrate these pages. We thank each of the following:

AGM-Urania/Koenigsfurt-Urania Verlag, Germany © ATM-Urania/ Koenigsfurt-Urania Verlag for permission to reproduce illustrations from *Vision Quest Tarot* and *Arcus Arcanum Tarot*. We appreciate the work of Gayan S. Winter and Jo Dosé in creating the *Vision Quest* deck, and of artist Hansrudi Waescher under the supervision of Gunter Hager in creating the *Arcus Arcanum Tarot*.

Anna Franklin, for her blessings on our extensive use of illustrations from her spectacular *Pagan Ways Tarot*.

Aunia Kahn, artist, and Russell J. Moon, author, for permission to include images from their unique *Silver Era Tarot*.

Beth Seilonen for permission to use some of her fanciful images from *Dream Raven Tarot*.

Courtney Weber for permission to reproduce the remarkable illustrations from the photographic deck *Tarot of the Boroughs* set in New York City.

Jasmine Beckett-Griffith, illustrator, and her collaborator author JR Rivera, for permission to include their delightful *Beautiful Creatures Tarot* in these pages.

Jude Simmons, illustrator in collaboration with Kooch Daniels from their wonderful *Teen Tarot* deck.

Marie White, for permission to use illustrations from the bold and powerful *Mary-El Tarot*.

11

Robert M. Place and Hermes Publications for permission to reproduce illustrations from his remarkable *The Tarot of the Sevenfold Mystery*, one of the first decks published in the twenty-first century.

Tom Schick, for permission to use illustrations from Major Tom Schick's *Tarot of Marseilles*, an imaginative modern takeoff on the original *Tarot de Marseilles*.

Yoav Ben-Dov's *CBD Tarot de Marseilles*, a restored reproduction of the traditional deck printed by Nicholas Conver in 1760.

And of course, we deeply appreciate the generosity of Schiffer Publishing Company, publisher of the cards by Franklin, Kahn, Seilonen, Beckett-Griffith, White, and Schick for granting permission for their use. We also thank Pete Schiffer for encouraging us to use illustrations from decks produced by other publishers as well.

Images by these artists are used as follows:
Introduction, Part Headings, and Epilogue:
JR Rivera, Jasmine Becket-Griffith;
Chapter 1: Yoav Ben-Dov;
Chapter 2: Tom Schick;
Chapter 3: Gayan Winter, Jo Dosé (UGM-Urania);
Chapter 4: Marie White;
Chapter 5: Hansrudi Waescher (UGM-Urania);
Chapter 6: Aunia Kahn;
Chapter 7: Robert Place;
Chapter 8: Courtney Weber plus two cards by Jude Simmons;
Chapter 9: Beth Seilonen;
Chapter 10: One card by Hansrudi Waescher;
Chapter 11, Jude Simmons;
Chapter 12: Anna Franklin;
Chapters 13, 14, and 15: one card each by Anna Franklin; and
Chapter 13 has four cards by Hansrudi Waescher.

With all chapters except 13-15, one card by the artist whose work illustrates the chapter is shown on its title page.
Our enormous gratitude and blessings to you all!

PREFACE

0. *The* EXPLORER

Sunlight and shadows, smooth sailing and stormy seas, challenges and opportunities—in one way or another all these are part of every person's life, of what it is to be human in this world. From time to time almost everyone runs aground on an unseen, unexpected reef—and needs a little help to navigate and to improve their chances of finding a speedy resolution. If you live in India you probably go to your spiritual teacher or guru for advice. If you live in the Western world, you might consult a counselor or psychotherapist to sort through life's lessons. Or depending on your background and beliefs, you might seek out a psychic, fortune-teller, or a personal coach. Or maybe you just tough it out by yourself, perhaps with a deck of Tarot cards in hand and the hope that they will help you find some sense of direction.

Whether your life journey involves being a healer for others, or trying to puzzle out a solution to your own dilemmas with a deck of Tarot, Lenormand, or oracular cards, we wrote this book for you. Perhaps you've studied to become a psychologist, psychotherapist, counselor, or social worker and you would like to use visual imagery in your work. Or you may be a Tarot reader seeking new perspectives on the cards. In either case, this book will lead you along paths toward unexpected destinations where unforeseen treasures are waiting to be discovered. It offers new techniques and methods that can augment the process you already use. You do not need previous Tarot experience or years of Tarot study to use the methods found here, but you do need to be willing to experience a nontraditional way of working with Tarot cards.

We wrote this book for two different primary audiences. One is Tarot readers who would like a broader psychological background and some new methods and insights to use in their readings.

The other audience is psychotherapists, counselors, and personal coaches who would like to integrate the use of visual imagery and the methods that accompany its use into their professional repertoires. (In this book we use the terms "psychotherapist" and "counselor" largely interchangeably.)

If you belong to neither of the groups just mentioned, but just enjoy using the cards for enjoyment, self-exploration, and personal growth, well, we wrote this book for you, too.

In writing for distinctly different audiences at once, we faced challenges. Some of the language used by Tarot readers and psychotherapists is different. Some of the methods described here are suitable for therapists but usually not Tarot readers, and vice-versa. We have tried to write from both mind and heart in ways that those in both the Tarot community and psychology world will find useful. We hope you enjoy the journey.

Using the Tarot in counseling or psychotherapy is fundamentally different from using it for divination, even though the underlying structure of the Tarot and its imagery lends itself well to use in both worlds. Traditionally, the Tarot, an ancient storybook of universal wisdom consisting of seventy-eight cards, has been associated with fortune-tellers, but it speaks to anyone who is interested in its pictorial vocabulary of images and symbols. In recent years it has become more widely accepted in mainstream society and the world of psychology. In response, we have been teaching psychotherapists and counselors how to use it to complement their work.

Enthusiastic responses from colleagues and students who have attended our presentations at psychotherapy conferences encouraged us to write a book for those who are intrigued by the possibilities of merging psychotherapy and the mystical. Although the Tarot is not for everyone, for those who appreciate its possibilities it holds vast potential for expanding awareness. Likewise, discussions with card readers at Tarot conferences made it clear that many would like to know how insights from psychology, psychotherapy, and counseling can improve and enrich their readings. Ruth Ann Amberstone, co-creator with her husband Wald, of New York's annual Reader's Studio and Tarot and Psychology conference, claims that we can use the Tarot to "map the true self." Her comment suggests that the Tarot can be useful to many different kinds of practitioners. Whatever your profession or trade, you can use Tarot imagery to find a pathway into the secret corridors of the self to help solve the puzzles of life and gain insight into mental, emotional, and relational problems and opportunities of many kinds.

Even though their approaches necessarily differ in basic ways, the Tarot reader and the therapist or other human services professional can learn from each other. Few psychologists know the complex meanings attached to the cards, whereas most readers go to great lengths to learn about each card's meanings and symbols. What does a specific card imply? What previously unseen avenues does it reveal?

Similarly, only a small number of readers have the professional training needed to delve deeply into people's emotional and relational issues. Someone can start reading the Tarot for the public as soon as he or she feels confident discussing the card's divinatory meanings. In most of the United States readers are required to either have a ministerial license or work as an entertainment service. In many countries and every US state, laws prohibit anyone from calling him or herself a "counselor" or "psychotherapist" and charging money for such services unless they have met specific licensing requirements. It takes specialized, accredited training to obtain such skill and such a license. But even for a person who has such professional training, the Tarot and other forms of imagery offers an additional way to uncover hidden dimensions of a client's issues.

We honor the obvious and subtle distinctions and boundaries of each of these different worlds. We are not trying to turn Tarot readers into psychologists or psychologists into Tarot readers—except for the determined few who wish to navigate through both realms.

Many who have spent years developing clinical and counseling skills are not going to spend the additional time needed to gain an in-depth knowledge of card meanings and their traditional symbolism. For instance, it can take years of study to learn to "read" cards in relation to their corresponding paths on the Kabalistic Tree of Life, their astrological correspondences, or their numerological or mythological relationships. With this in mind, if you would like to use the Tarot in your therapeutic or counseling practice, you may benefit from using the cards in a *representational* manner. You can learn this approach in the chapters that follow. It involves encouraging your clients to respond spontaneously to whatever personal meanings particular card images evoke. This contrasts with traditional methods used by Tarot readers, who use the cards in a *divinatory* manner. We also show how sometimes the Tarot can be used in both representational and divinatory ways within a single reading or therapy session, such as when you want to encourage a person's creativity.

We do not explore the history of the Tarot in great depth or discuss card interpretations at great length because you can find such information in conventional Tarot books and websites. However, in the final four chapters we do provide examples of divinatory meanings, key words, and phrases that you might use with the cards.

Please note that we are not advising you to discontinue previous Tarot studies. We offer our representational method as one path to using the cards that differs from the well-known path of learning traditional symbolic interpretation. It can supplement divinatory readings or be used in place of them.

The Deck

If you already use the Tarot, you doubtless have a deck, or even a collection of them. If you're just starting to get interested and don't already have a deck, you'll need one. A variety of decks, both modern and traditional, can be found in most bookstores, or online sites such as Schiffer Publishing (www.schifferbooks.com). You will want to look at the cards in several (or many) different decks to find one that you will enjoy using. Although styles and colors differ, we suggest getting a traditional deck with seventy-eight cards, including the twenty-two Major Arcana cards and the fifty-six Minor Arcana cards. The latter group includes each of four suits: Cups, Wands, Swords, and Pentacles. But you may notice that the names of the suits in some decks differ, such as Staves or Rods or Fire instead of Wands; Crystals or Air instead of Swords; Water or Chalices instead of Cups; and Disks or Coins or Earth instead of Pentacles.

If you don't already know the card names, you can look at a book that uses the images in the ubiquitous *Rider Waite Coleman Smith Deck* or the *Thoth Tarot Deck* by Aleister Crowley to view their long-established titles. Whatever deck you choose, as long as it follows the customary format and titles for the twenty-two Major Arcana cards and four suits you will be able to easily follow along with our Tarot discussions, and practice the techniques we offer. But that's just our suggestion, since those cards and images are keyed directly to the text of this book. If you prefer the imagery of a different kind of deck such as an oracle deck that has a different number of cards, the methods described here can work equally well for you.

When selecting a Tarot deck, be sure to choose one that is rich in imagery in all seventy-eight cards. In some decks, the cards representing the Minor Arcana have only numbers and icons for each suit, but no pictorial image. Such cards may work well for divination, but are less useful for representational card sessions.

Also, when following the methods described here, we usually recommend avoiding decks that have words other than the card titles printed on the cards to describe their import, such as "problems," "decisions," "marriage," etc. Such labels can interfere with your client's selection of personal meanings for the card's images.

When you first get your deck, find a nice-looking box or cloth bag to put it in that will help you handle the cards with loving care and protect them from damage. With your deck in hand, you'll soon be ready to experience using the methods in the following pages to open doorways to new perceptions and exciting possibilities.

1 *of* AIRS

PART I

Infinite Possibilities Beckon

LE·MONDE

1.

TAROT AND PSYCHOTHERAPY THEN AND NOW

Jennifer wanted to know whether she was going to find love. Could the cards tell her? Time after time, she would meet someone interesting, they would have a few dates, and then somehow the relationship would sputter and trail off. What might the future hold?

When thinking about the Tarot, most people envision fortune-tellers who can read the cards and say something about their futures. Such Tarot readings, whether in a private consulting session, given quickly by a reader at a party, or even over the phone on a "psychic hotline," are all divinatory readings. The reader is trying to enrich a person's perspectives and divine something about the other person's life or their future, whether regarding love, money, career, family, health, or some other concern.

Many readers are very good at understanding how to do this, since they study many years, attend professional Tarot conferences, and are continually trying to sharpen their skills. They consult various traditions as they develop their own methods of helping people address important questions.

In a divinatory session, some of these methods involve the reader shuffling the cards or having the other person do so. During the shuffle the reader has the option of asking the person to think silently about what is most important in their life at present. Or, he or she might ask the person why they have come for a reading. What questions might they explore that would be most valuable? If a person does intuitive Tarot readings, he or she might not want the person to verbalize their concerns, as the reader will let the cards and the client's dominant energy point to the most beneficial message. Some people sit down for a reading because the opportunity is there and they've never had a reading before. In reply to, "Do you have a specific question that you want the reading to address, or would you just like to see what story your cards tell?" many choose the last alternative.

A reader has many options about which deck to use since a multitude of them exist. Even most modern decks follow the general outlines of the early hand-painted ones that date back to Renaissance Italy during the 1400s before the invention of the printing press.

The Tarot began to move toward its present form during the first half of the fifteenth century. Card decks were being developed in Italy, in Milan, Ferrara, Bologna, and perhaps other cities, too. Old records mention a hand-painted deck of playing cards called *Imperatori* in the early 1400's.[1] Another candidate for the oldest deck is the *Michelino* Deck produced between 1417 and 1425, commissioned by Filippo Maria Visconti, duke of Milano, a card lover who is also credited with designing the *Tarocchi* game playing cards. Italy is still one of the world's hotbeds of Tarot card production and activity.

A work published in 1506, written by Raphaeus Maffei or Raphaelis Volaterraini described the trump cards or *atouts* as:

The Fool	The Juggler	Pope Joan	The Pope
The Empress	The Emperor	Love	The Chariot
Courage	The Old Man	The Wheel	Justice
The Hanged Man	Death	Temperance	The Devil
Fire	The Star	The Moon	The Sun
The Angel	Justice	The World[2]	

Dr. Yoav Ben-Dov, a psychotherapist and organizational consultant, writes that in the 1700s and 1800s card makers in France, and especially Marseilles, adopted a common model for Tarot decks that became a standard that has endured until our own time. The *Tarot de Marseilles*, printed by Nicholas Conver in 1760, was the first mass-produced deck, in contrast to the decks hand-painted for wealthy patrons and the copper engravings by Andrea Mantegna that preceded it. Ben-Dov has created a faithful reproduction of Conver's deck, now widely available as the *CBD Tarot de Marseille*.[3] Shown here are three cards from the CBD re-creation of the original deck: The Chariot, The Tower, and the Queen of Swords.

Psychotherapy and counseling as we know them today have more recent histories. They began to be seriously explored only near the end of the nineteenth century and the start of the twentieth. Mention the word "psychiatry" or "psychoanalysis" and a picture of Sigmund Freud sitting near a couch on which a patient is reclining is likely to pop into a person's mind. In the US, but not all countries, psychoanalysis and psychiatry have in common the requirement that the practitioner have an MD, which allows them to prescribe medication as a treatment for problems. Most psychotherapists and counselors, however, are neither psychoanalysts nor psychiatrists.[4]

Interestingly, even in Freud's day only psychoanalysts used "the couch." Other renowned practitioners such as Carl Jung and Alfred Adler sat face-to face with their clients. As time passed, the couch fell from favor among all but psychoanalysts, and by the 1950s and 1960s, even some of them began to sit facing their clients.

From Observable Behavior to the Depths of the Psyche

Some early twentieth century psychotherapists were interested in the unseen inner events that inspired a person's words and actions. Others, aspiring to be just as scientific as a physicist or chemist, confined their observations to actions that could be seen or measured. They looked askance at all actions that could not be quantified in some fashion. After several decades, however, these "behaviorists" found that people did many things that their methods and instruments simply could not address.

In the meantime, Sigmund Freud, Carl Jung, and others continued to be interested in hidden events and messages that lurked in the subterranean chambers of the mind. These included deeply buried feelings and impulses, and unknown and underdeveloped sides of the self. They believed that only when people come to know the deep currents of their consciousness can they deal with life's problems well.

In the mid-twentieth century, new methods emerged among therapists who focused on the inner storylines of what their clients told them. Person-centered therapist Carl Rogers, psychodramatist Jacob Moreno, and gestalt therapist Fritz Perls were central figures in these new developments. They paid close attention to posture, gestures, muscular tightening, and relaxation, lines in the face, tones of voice, and modes of sitting, standing, and moving. They sought to help a client become aware of patterns of behavior that were outside their awareness. They developed ways to help clients look at mental snapshots and mind-movies that they had been keeping out of their consciousness because they seemed scary or embarrassing. Starting at the surface, such therapists gradually guided clients into the depths of their psyches, and some would even say, their souls. Meanwhile, psychoanalyst Wilhelm Reichs brought attention to the physical body into psychological work for the first time.

Early on, Carl Jung had his patients draw and use artistic media to express themselves in ways that they could not quite do in words. One of his Swiss colleagues, Dora Kalff, along with Margaret Lowenfeld in England, developed a working/playing method called sand tray therapy that gave tangible form to mental images. Still in use today, it helps both children and adults express their unspoken thoughts and emotions. The client selects tiny doll figures to represent people and events in their lives and stands them upright in a box of sand. Then the client is asked to have them talk to each other and act in ways that reflect their issues. Because such a dialogue is projected from the client's imagination, it can be called a *projective dialogue*.

Jung was not the only practitioner to use artistic media. Eventually a whole specialty of "art therapy" came into being. Other psychotherapists, taking a clue from drama and theater, set up a "stage" on which patients could act out their thoughts, feelings, and impulses. The favored term for people undergoing psychotherapy and counseling changed from "patients" to "clients" in the mind-twentieth century, thanks to Carl Rogers' widespread influence. The best known of the drama-oriented practitioners was Jacob Moreno, founder of psychodrama.

During the 1950s, Fritz Perls, a psychoanalyst with a background in theater and his wife, Laura, who had trained with experimental psychologists of the gestalt school[5] joined forces with psychologists Paul Goodman and Ralph Hefferline in New York. They developed a method that blended elements from traditional psychotherapies with elements of Moreno's psychodramatic work. A crucial difference between their approach and Moreno's is that in psychodrama the client, working in a group setting, chooses other group members to act out the roles of those involved in

a problem situation, while in gestalt therapy the client acts out all the different roles. Perls placed an unoccupied chair in front of the one occupied by the client, labeled it the "empty chair," and called the one in which the client was sitting the "hot seat." However, not all gestalt therapists use these labels, or these enactive methods.

Artistic media, the sand tray with its many shelves of figurines, and the hot seat and empty chair(s) all have a limitation: They are not so easy to move around. On the other hand, a deck of cards is completely portable.

The Unexpected Meeting of Psychotherapy and the Tarot

In the past the Tarot has been used mainly as a divinatory oracle. Now, as its popularity grows and it has become more accepted by mainstream society, its usefulness as a healing tool is becoming recognized. More than a decade ago we began exploring the therapeutic potential of Tarot cards. We already knew their images could illuminate a broad spectrum

of dilemmas, vices, virtues, cravings, and opportunities. We have found that pictorial imagery—especially Tarot cards—support the telling of emotionally loaded stories and memories. They can be used in a one-time session or repeatedly in ongoing sessions over a period of time.

Gradually we realized that some of the processes used in gestalt therapy can also be used with the cards. At first we worked with cards that clients pulled from a deck in a traditional divinatory manner. Eventually we found that often it makes sense to spread the deck face up in front of your client and let him or her choose cards to represent particular people, situations, or sides of himself or herself. With minor adaptations, projective dialogues like those used in sand tray work, the hot seat, and empty chair style of working, can easily be carried out by a client using Tarot cards.

Also, the use of Tarot images is at least distantly related to the Rorschach inkblot test, created by Hermann Rorschach in 1920, to

diagnose personality problems. The Thematic Apperception Test (TAT) devised by Henry Murray and Christiana Morgan in 1930 serves a related purpose. In a somewhat similar manner, some Tarot readers are trained to use the images on the cards to analyze their querent's perceptions and discuss their potentials. Much of most people's thinking occurs in the forms of mental pictures and mind-movies. To limit therapeutic intervention to verbal conversation neglects that vast realm of personal experience. Given the picture and mental-movie character of so much of people's thinking in both dreaming and waking states, it makes perfect sense that visual imagery is beginning to catch on in the study of the mind.

After presenting our methods at several psychotherapy conferences, we gave a talk and demonstration on using the cards for therapy at the Reader's Studio "Psychology and Tarot" Conference in New York City in April of 2014. Afterward one of the participants, Dr. Yoav Ben-Dov, told us that Tarot and other imagery cards have been used in psychotherapy in Israel for about fifteen years by Dr. Ofra Ayalon, especially for healing post-traumatic stress. He himself uses them in organizational consulting. When people in a group share their differing associations to card images, it can open up channels of communication and contact that are otherwise hard to access.

Our experience suggests that the use of evocative imagery in psychotherapy, and some of the relevant knowledge and practice by Tarot readers, can combine seamlessly to bring new understandings of how to use the cards. Beyond question this is already happening.

Doing Tarot Divination vs. Tarot Counseling and Therapy

For the most part when we place our central focus on using the cards in psychotherapy or counseling, traditional interpretation is tossed out the window. Instead of having a reading, the client undertakes a journey of self-discovery in which he or she attributes subjective meanings to the cards. Such personally assigned associations may be quite different from the meanings another client, or the counselor, or a Tarot reader would suggest. A gestalt approach also emphasizes paying attention to developing greater awareness of feelings, thoughts, and sensations in the present moment. Such direct experience of the self in "the here and now" in reaction to card images is quite different from traditional divinatory interpretation.

The lines of distinction between Tarot readers and licensed counselors and therapists can and usually should be clearly defined. Upon occasion, however, they can blur. A Tarot reader is sometimes called upon to play the role of a therapist, particularly by people who refuse to see a therapist or counselor because they think it means there "must be something wrong with them" if they do. They may, however, think it's "fun and interesting" to go to a reader to address the same issues that others would take to a counselor or therapist. And sometimes a therapist is called upon to act like a reader and offer suggestions pertaining to the future— although many therapists are wary about "giving advice." Practical training and methods used by readers, counselors, and other healers may vary, but the following list offers some perspective on this sensitive subject.

Some Differences & Similarities between Divination & Representational Use of the Tarot

DIVINATORY USE	REPRESENTATIONAL USE
Offered by Tarot reader	Offered by counselor or clinician
Tarot is an effective point of contact	Tarot is an effective point of contact
Meets needs of querent	Meets needs of client
Extensive Tarot knowledge, experience, and intuition guide readings	Therapeutic training and experience and sometimes intuition guide session(s)
Querent picks cards "blind" from a face-down deck	Client selects specific cards from a face-up deck
Emphasis is on traditional card meanings	Emphasis is on client's reactions to cards
Reader lays spreads and leads discussion	Therapist lets client spark key points

Here is a sample of the vocabulary that you're likely to hear if you listen to readers or psychologists talking:

The Spoken Word

MORE LIKELY TO HEAR DURING DIVINATION	MORE LIKELY TO HEAR IN THERAPY OR COUNSELING
Healing	Therapeutic session
Karma	Conflict
Self-discovery	Self-actualization
Thinking	Cognition
Knowing	Awareness
Spiritual	Transpersonal
Physical	Somatic
Aura	Field
Affirmations	Guided imagery
Divine Guidance	Synchronicity

Just as vocabularies differ, many people disagree about who has the better understanding of how to use the cards in a specific context. But history has seen worse. In the fourteenth century, in parts of Europe, there was actually a prohibition denying people the right to use playing cards. And believe it or not, even today in the US state of North Carolina, the "Anti-Divination Law" prohibits publicly practicing the art of Tarot reading.

There will probably always be people who argue with the merits of any system of thought, just as there are differences between (and sometimes even within) schools of psychotherapy. Differences of opinion are a normal part of life, but in the worlds of "readers" and "psychologists," both consist of people who are working to heal the hurts of humanity. Both have a right to use the best approaches they can find that will make positive differences in people's lives. The question at stake is the effectiveness and outcome of the work being done.

Connecting with Meaningful Images: Creating Your Own Tarot Card

We'd like to suggest that you take some time to notice how you personally connect with and experience visual imagery, and to reflect on which images are important in your life. You can do this in part by thinking about the impact of photos or art in advertisements, videos, or magazines that grab your attention. Look inward and notice the visual mental images that you see in your mind's eye or dreams. Which images do you see as "good" or beautiful and which do you see as "bad" or distasteful? What does your selection of art reveal about you?

Some years ago we offered a college course on the Tarot in which each student's work included making a Tarot card of his or her own choosing in a collage-like format. The results were stunning. The visual images on the cards spoke directly from the hearts of the designers.

To help you connect with the power of images, we suggest that you create your own Tarot card(s) using a collage technique. You may or may not want to start by finding words that express a meaningful message for your card. You can pick from traditional Tarot card titles or make up ones that suit your taste and present mood. Once you've decided on your card's title, the theme for your card's art will naturally reveal itself. After that, you can move into production mode. Gather interesting and meaningful clips of personal photos, art, or newspaper or magazine clippings, or free, public domain digital downloads or words. You can type or handwrite your own soul-touching messages on your card. Or you can do the same thing with a drawing or photo program on a computer screen.

If you're using paper instead of a computer to do your art, find some glue and assemble your collage by putting together your collection of artist clips, drawings, and messages in a meaningful pattern on a piece of cardstock or canvas. The size and background color of your card is your choice.

Once finished, stand back and look at your collage. What does it seem to say? Take as long as you need to reflect on what messages both its individual pieces and the whole card may hold for you. Some of its parts may speak to you in a different way than they did before they became part of the collage. After all, as Max Wertheimer, the founder of gestalt psychology said, "The whole is different from the sum of its parts."

Next we will look at some specific ways of using the cards that can be useful for the whole porridge pot of psychotherapists, counselors, personal coaches, Tarot readers, and anyone else who wants to experience more of the powerful possibilities contained within them.

CAVALIER OF BATONS

2.

WHAT DOES EACH CARD SAY TO YOU?

Every new student of the Tarot wonders about the best way to learn to use the cards. Although there are various ways to work and play with the Tarot, a few suggestions can help no matter how you want to use them.

When we ask therapists whether they would like to try using the Tarot in their work, a common reply is, "Yes, but I don't know the meanings of the cards and I don't have time to study them." Of course it would be wonderful if we all had unlimited time to read and study any subject that captures our interest, but most of us have a long list of responsibilities and stacks of bills to pay. Amid the consuming job of building our careers, we seldom have enough time to develop all of our interests.

If you don't have time to learn seventy-eight card meanings as you juggle personal and professional demands, but you'd like to include the Tarot in your practice, the following suggestions can help you learn to discuss card associations without formal study. You'll need to invest some time in practicing or "playing" with your deck, but you can learn at your own pace. This course of study does not require a structured time frame. You can follow the suggestions below whenever you feel inspired to look at your cards, or even when you just need a break from your everyday concerns.

With a little effort and the wish to succeed, you will learn the art of card reading. It's important to replace most "I can't" doubts that you might have with a positive approach, like "I can do this." Building Tarot expertise results from the desire and willingness to learn from your experience with the cards. Your response to a card's image and making note of what you feel, sense, or see in its symbols is a splendid teacher.

XII – THE HANGED MAN   CAVALIER OF COINS   QUEEN OF SWORDS

Don't expect to become a master of the cards overnight. Day by day you'll learn about them through your personal experience and reflections. You might even start right now. Take a minute or two to look at each of the three cards from Major Tom's unique *Tarot of Marseilles Deck* that follows. While you're looking at them, see if you find a message or insight that has some value for you in one or more of them. Noticing your reactions to them is a start to learning something about them.

XI – STRENGTH

Viewing the Cards in Different Ways

To show two very different ways of working with the cards, we offer the following analysis of the Major Arcana card "Strength," comparing a traditional interpretation of this card and a representational reading. The two ways of viewing this card demonstrate some of the differences between viewing a card through its potential divinatory meanings and exploring it as a reflection of your own or your client's personal experiences and associations. At this point we're not describing methods of using the cards in therapy or counseling or divination. We're talking about getting a sense of what the card is about.

First, here is our short version of a more traditional interpretation of the Major Arcana card Strength. This card, attributed by Kabalists to *Teth*, the ninth letter of the Hebrew Alphabet connected with the mystery of the Tree of Knowledge, is numbered eight in the *Rider Waite Coleman Smith Deck* and numbered eleven in the *Tarot of Marseille*. This card has the privilege of being placed in different positions depending on the esoteric orientation of the deck creator.

Above the maiden's head is a lemniscate, the visual symbol for infinity that looks like the number eight lying on its side. In this deck, it forms the brim of her hat. Besides suggesting infinite possibilities, it also refers to the universal balance of action and reaction, giving and receiving, eternity in the now. Additionally, it tells us that this card's figure, (in most decks a maiden) has vitality and fortitude connected to transcendent, unconditional all-loving consciousness. By calming and closing the mouth of the lion, (or is she opening it?), the maiden shows discipline over untamed instincts. Her compassion and courage is the power that conquers fear.

Also, the majestic lion, symbol for the Sun sign Leo, celestial royalty of the stars, cosmically points to a connection with the fifth zodiac house and the heart, spine, creativity and children. The only astrological sign ruled by the Sun, Leo symbolizes a potent force that helps us take a winning approach to life and conquer challenges by turning them into positive experiences. This reflects a harmonious connection between dominance and submission when love is the ruling force. Common key meanings for this card are having or developing the strength to overcome obstacles, finding the courage to love or to use your creativity, and getting in touch with your personal power or will to succeed. As we will see, however, depending on the querent or client, it might mean something very different. A symbol needs to be interpreted in a way that fits a person's situation and present attitude in life.

All this may seem like a lot to digest, perhaps because the card description above requires some knowledge of both astrology and the Kabbalah. Not all Tarot readers use astrology or discuss the Kabbalah, (depending on your inclinations, you can research them or not), but as you study the cards you will surely come across interpretations that include various mystical correlations and their age-old astrological connections.

A Different Kind of Interpretation

Now by contrast, here is a sample interpretation of the Strength card viewing it through a looking glass of personal experience. We are imagining that the viewer has never seen the card and has no understanding of traditional card meanings. The comments below are an impromptu response to the question: "What do you see in the card?"

After viewing the card silently for several minutes the client replies:

> I love the word "strength." It reminds me to strive to be more confident and assertive. The woman is brave enough to straddle a lion. I wish I could be that strong instead of running away from whatever makes me nervous. I'm sure my love life would be better if I didn't panic and run because I'm afraid I'll be rejected. If I could be more like the woman in that card, I wouldn't let my vulnerability overrule my confidence and trust. I see an infinity symbol above her head that makes me think she's a spiritual being. Perhaps this card has something to do with the Hindu goddess of strength, Durga, who rides the lion. Because I see so much yellow, it makes me think of a sunny day and feel hopeful. The reddish-brown mane makes me think of being fiery and adventurous. And of Carl Jung's *Red Book*. Some of these symbols I've even seen in my dreams.

These reactions are more personal than the traditional meanings for the Strength card. When two people are asked to share their personal associations, they might have opposite, or nearly opposite, responses to the same card. In a nontraditional reading, there are no rules or "shoulds" about a card's symbolism. Its meaning comes alive in the moment that it triggers something important in the person getting the reading.

The Role of Numbers

In divinatory readings, people often ask about the meaning of the numbers on the cards. We go into that deeply in Chapter Fourteen. For now, you might reflect on how you relate to different numbers. For example: What is your lucky number? Do you have an unlucky number? Are some numbers more important to you than others? Why? You can make a list with the numbers 1 to 10. Next to each number write a few words describing your association to it. For example:

One: "I'm number one, the first!"
Two: "Me and my boyfriend make two; relationships."
Three: "My favorite number."
Four: "Four equal sides make a square."
Five: "I have five keys."
Six: "Six is sex-y."
Seven: "My winning number."
Eight: "Lucky number of good fortune for the Chinese."
Nine: "I'm taking nine classes."
Ten: "Reminds me of the month I was born, October."

Without learning numerology, you can reflect on your personal numeric associations. They will filter into your readings and card discussions.

Thinking about your associations with colors can be equally useful. What pops into your mind when you see the color blue, or for that matter any other color? Because color is on every card, unless you are using a black and white deck, it becomes one measure for how you feel in relation to viewing an image. If you are so inclined, you can make a list of colors in one column and then note your associations with each in a parallel column. Soon you will find that this simple exercise benefits your practice. Here are two examples of linking feelings with color:

• Red is often associated with blood, the life force, and heat of passion; also anger.
• Blue is frequently connected to the sky, and expansiveness, and the flow of emotions.

When the time seems right, you can continue thinking about how you associate each color with feelings and ideas.

Three Essential Keys to Learning the Tarot

- Be patient with your progress.
- Invoke your inner optimist.
- Practice, and have fun!

Learning Each Card's Meaning

When some people who want to use the cards for divination begin to learn the Tarot, they start solely with the twenty-two Major cards. There are so many Minor Arcana cards that learning all fifty-six of them can be daunting. However, if you intend to do representational counseling, therapy, or readings as described in the coming chapters, you don't need to memorize the card's meanings and it will help your work to use your entire deck.

KING OF BATONS

III – THE EMPRESS

It's useful to have your cards nearby when you read this section so that you can practice with them as you consider the following ideas. The suggested activities offer ways to obtain personal insights into the cards without referring to any customary "How to Read the Tarot" manual. Letting your thoughts be your guide, you'll learn about the cards through your own associations to them.

Twelve Activities to Help You Design Your Tarot Environment

1. Make a daily or weekly practice of placing a card on your dresser and causally glance at it as you walk by. You might even dialogue with it. What does it say to you? What is most interesting about it or most important to you at that moment?

2. Free-associate any meanings that you connect with each card. Does the image remind you of anyone you know, or any event or situation? Does anything seem unusual or contradictory in a way that might point to hidden currents of thought or feeling? You might even try this suggestion with either the King of Batons or the Empress from Major Tom's deck right now!

3. Find the symbols and colors in each card that stand out to you. Also look at what forms leap out from a card's background. What do you associate with these images?

4. Does any other aspect of a card, such as title or gender, offer clues to possible meanings for you?

5. What message does each card personally send to you?

6. Reflect on the moods evoked in you as you view a card. Do you find anything amusing, distressing, confusing, or perplexing?

7. Embody the statement you find in the card in your posture, gestures, movements, voice, or all of the above. Imagine that you are that statement. What does your body tell you? What do you discover or uncover about yourself and/or the card?

8. Place two cards side-by-side and look at their differences and similarities. Do the figures look at one another or do they look away? What might they be looking at? How do they relate or "speak" to one another? Again, here are two more cards so you can try this now:

KING OF COINS

QUEEN OF CUPS

37

9. Notice when you find the same symbol in more than one card. Are the cards that share the same symbol linked in any way? If so, how? (Anything that seems to you to be a symbol can be one for you.)

10. Do you recognize any legend, universal meaning, archetype, or dream that might be connected with an image on the card?

11. Meditate on one card at a time. What do you feel or observe emotionally or mentally?

12. Keep a Tarot journal (see section that follows).

Your Personal Experience of the Cards

Perhaps viewing a card brings up memories that make you want to dance or go outside for a walk. Maybe a card gives you a feeling that suggests putting your cards away for now. Be open-minded and flexible about your reactions. No one else is an authority about how an image makes you feel. No reaction to a card is wrong. Let your own voice, whether it be confident or shaky, tell the unique story of how you personally relate to each card's imagery, symbolism, and possible implications.

Keeping a Tarot Journal

In a Tarot journal, if it pleases you to keep one, you can make note of your spontaneous experiences and associations with each card. Does a card inspire you, puzzle you, or make you feel anxious? Write down your reactions and reflections. Perhaps you'd like to write a poem about the images on a card or explain why you like or dislike a certain one. If you enjoy crafting, you can cut words, phrases, or pictures out of a magazine or newspaper that embody your responses and paste them into your journal.

Don't imagine that a journal entry has to be long. It might be, if you feel so inclined. Or you might have a passing thought that takes only a few words or lines to record. Sometimes just one sentence can capture the essence of an idea or insight. Give each entry a brief title that will stand out when you look back through the journal. In the future, just scanning through the titles may be useful to you.

There are many possible items to include in your journal. If you record your first reactions to a card or its title, you are almost guaranteed to be surprised when in the future you look back and read them. Your feelings evoked by the images are likely to develop and change once you have more experience with the cards. When you include your personal reactions in your journal, you'll be witnessing how your life evolves in time. The overall theme of your writing will be colored by the moods of your internal dialogues. Tarot images or symbols that appear in your dreams capture subconscious insights that you may want to remember. You can journal about any of your thoughts concerning emotional, psychic, spiritual, or other connections you notice or think are important. If you wish, you can make notations about:

- What your intuition tells you about each card.
- What your logic tells you about a card.
- The ways a card speaks to your heart.
- How an image inspires a past memory, future hope, or a spiritual or magical feeling.
- How a card helps you cultivate a relationship with your inner self.
- Whatever else occurs to you.

There isn't any "must include" list. Instead of writing with a pen, you can use colored pencils, paints, stamp art, or a keyboard or keypad. Instead of writing in prose, you can write in outline form. You can include what you wish and organize your ideas in any way that makes sense. You don't have to follow the organization of ideas that we present here. Your journal is your own creation and it lets you review your unique journey with the Tarot. You will be expanding your awareness each time you write and read what you've written.

Also, when you are beyond the initial stage of learning about each card and are doing readings or counseling for yourself or others, you can follow the guidelines we've suggested and take notes about what was most significant during a session. You might want to draw a picture, or take notes that describe your reaction to a card. What stood out? What evoked the strongest energy? What unique life experiences were discussed? Your journal can become a treasure house of personal history, your secret diary, and unique slant on life that you may enjoy looking at for years to come.

The following example illustrates a weekly entry for Jennifer, whom we met at the beginning of Chapter One:

Journal Notes
Date and time of reading: *2/3/15 @ 11:30 a.m.*
Place: *New Age Fair*
Name of person getting reading: *Jennifer Robins*
Age: *42*
Divinatory or Representational Session: *Div*
What cards were drawn? *The Lover, Valet of Coins, Wheel of Fortune*
How were they placed on the table? *In a straight row.*
What topics were discussed? *Stressful communications with boyfriend as another woman tries to lure him away.*

Noteworthy Information: *Jennifer seemed to open up and discuss her emotions when we began to compare her relationship to the images of the male and females on the Lover card. She especially liked the image of the Valet of Coins. She left the reading wanting to strengthen and heal their communications and open up a richer relational world instead of feeling hopeless about her connection with a man she described as "looks hot, but feels cool to the touch."*

My reaction: *Jen's story evolved quickly once we started discussing what the cards meant to her in relation to her love life.*

You might want to photocopy blank copies of the journal template found in Appendix 1, or electronically cut and paste them, or create your own journal template and then make copies. Create the journal that will be most useful to you.

If you don't want to journal, don't worry. It's not a "have to do." Follow your Tarot journey wherever it takes you. Be confident that you are gaining something each time you explore the meaning of a card. Your personal path evolves as you follow your passion and your own inclinations about how to proceed.

Now we move to looking at the character of the relationship between a querent or client and a reader or counselor. Whether in a brief reading or long-term therapeutic work, noticing the character of this relationship can have great value. When a person transfers thoughts and feelings from a past relationship onto a present one, it can interfere with an accurate perception of reality. What are some specific dimensions of this? Turn the page to see how cards can become springboards for discussing emotional perceptions.

3.

TRANSFERENCE: WHO IS THERE WITH YOU?

XX
Spirit Guide

Martha and Al, who just celebrated their first anniversary, are having relationship problems. Martha acts toward Al in some of the ways she used to act toward her first husband Jim, and she thinks that some of Al's mannerisms and expressions mean the same thing Jim meant by them. When Jim said, "I'm going to town this afternoon," it meant "I'm going out by myself and I don't care for company." When Al says, "I'm going out," she assumes that he means the same thing and she feels uncared for, even though he usually means, "and I'd be glad to have you come along, too." A couple's reading or counseling session with Al and Martha that uses card imagery in a representational manner can be a starting point with such misunderstandings.

On occasion when we meet someone, consciously or unconsciously, they remind us of someone we knew in an earlier period of our life—or maybe even last week. As a result, we may feel and act toward them as we felt and acted toward the person in our past. We imagine that they think and feel as that old acquaintance (or boss or spouse or lover) would have thought or felt. A similar dynamic can actually be a valuable, and sometimes even essential, part of a reading or therapeutic session. Close attention to how a person makes contact, watching and hearing whether the person responds to "others" as they really are instead of partly confusing their perceptions of them with figures ("ghosts") from their past is a useful tactic.

There is a saying that when a couple comes in for counseling, there are at least six people in the room: the couple and both of each partner's parents. Add the counselor or reader and that makes seven. Depending on the person's life history, in single-parent families or those with multiple parental figures, there may be fewer people, or more.

Sigmund Freud made such observations a central focus of his approach. His concept of "transference" assumed that each patient transfers their mental and emotional responses to one or more important people from their past or present life onto the psychoanalyst. As the relationship between client and analyst evolves, gradually the person learns to respond to the analyst in realistic ways and then take those new ways of relating into interactions with others. You might not have the luxury of the time that such a process sometimes takes. Nonetheless, a person's responses to you, and yours to him or her, can profoundly affect the character, quality, and success of your work.

In traditional psychoanalysis, the term "transference" refers just to the patient's projections and actions in regard to the analyst. But actually, almost everyone engages in transference toward a spectrum of people in their lives. As you saw with Martha and Al, this is often an issue in marriage and many other relationships.

When a person walks into your consulting room or up to your table, note your first impressions. Right from the start of your first encounter pay attention to how the person relates to you from that moment until the end of the session: warmly and openly, or as an all-knowing authority, or in a guarded and suspicious way, or a tightly controlled manner? Is his or her manner importuning, seductive, authoritarian, skeptical, obsequious, cool, or warm? What does that suggest about the implications of the cards you pull? What strengths or deficiencies in communication and other social skills do you feel in the connection between you that occurs during your time together? That probably offers clues to his or her way of being with other people, too. Shyness, or fear of looking directly into your eyes, is information that can help you expand the insights that come from his or her comments. It also gives you clues about this person's likely issues and strengths in relationships with others. It offers guidance about how you might best guide your work together.

There is, of course, the delicate matter of what lies hidden inside the mind. Some of what you see and hear on the outside will be different from a person's interior reality. Carl Jung called our facial expressions and behavioral patterns that we display to others "the persona." Many people never really learn that what others wear on their face for the public eye to see may hide very different feelings, emotions, and motives that lie lurking in their depths, but reactions to the card imagery will often help reveal the underlying realities.

Also it's important to take a few moments to check inwardly with yourself. What thoughts and feelings are stirred in you by this person's manner? Do you feel drawn to help a needy soul, inclined to be reserved and distant, or what? In psychological language, this is the *counter-transference*. Every reader, counselor, or psychotherapist has his or her own interests, inclinations, beliefs, attitudes, and even prejudices. All these affect what happens in a session.

The responses that a person triggers in you may be much like those that he or she tends to trigger in others. With due discretion on your part, sharing how you respond, or mentioning what you see or feel in this person's behavior, may make a valuable contribution to your discussion. Conversely, if a person is overly sensitive, he or she might be alarmed by such straightforwardness, and become guarded. Your in-the-now intuition about how to best communicate with someone is often your most trustworthy guide.

You can also learn from the way a person communicates. The particular words being shared and how they are being used can be a treasure chest of useful information. For instance, when you notice that someone makes a comment, and then quickly moves away from it, that can be a signal that points to a crucial "What happened?" question. Here's a real life example. The client, Anita, had selected the "Transformation" card from a face-up *Vision Quest Deck* (in most decks the equivalent card is called "Death") and was speaking of the hard time she had discussing deep feeling with her father. She moved to a brief comment about her sister, and then returned to her father.

XIII
Transformation

Therapist: "You mentioned a few words about your sister and then quickly jumped back to talking about your father. What happened with your sister?"

Client: [Hesitation . . . then] "She . . . she overdosed on drugs and died last year. She was my best friend."

This comment was a signal for the central work of the session to begin. The discussion we had been having about the woman's insensitive father vanished in a cloud of smoke and the rest of our time dealt with the client's relationship with her sister.

Listening to hear the quality and character of any comment, especially unusual ones, is also helpful. It may alter the tone of the discussion about what the cards mean to that person. Often it's important to encourage even a simple response, "Yes, that fits," or even, "and it reminds me of . . . " Or alternatively, "No, that's off the mark for me, but what your comment does point to is . . . " In either case, any personal response, whether framed as an observation, a guess, a hypothesis, or an imagined scenario, opens up a broad channel of communication and awareness that goes beyond a simple answer.

The Querent or Client and You

What signs do you usually look for in others that tell you something about the attitude exhibited toward life, you, and probably at least some others as well? The following brief activity can make the above question more concrete. If you're willing, try this right now.

Think about the conscious and unconscious signs and signals people offer to give you information about them. You can do this from memory, but don't use vague generalities like "reading their energy," "body language" or "paralanguage." ("*Paralanguage* is a term that includes tone of voice, choice of language, and patterns of movement"). Be specific.

Here are two examples:
- She sticks out her chest, pulls her shoulders upward into a high, rigid position, and in a parody of exaggerated power, peppers her comments with profanity.
- He looks downward, avoiding eye contact, speaks in a low voice that sounds almost choked, and repeatedly gestures with open palms facing upward that seem to say, "but I've no idea what I could do about it."

Take pen and paper or open your Tarot journal or a note-taking file, and jot down two or more examples of your own. Base these on your own remembered observations and experiences. Or go out for a walk and observe people. What nonverbal signals alerted—or alert—you to each person's state of mind?

Now, what are at least two signals you notice in yourself that may tell you something about your own reactions to someone who sits down at your table or walks into your office? Do you have trigger points that affect your reactions? If so, how do you react, and how do these reactions tend to affect the way your querent or client responds to you?

Again, take time to think and then jot down several examples. If examples don't come easily, then start to notice your own internal and external behavior with others more attentively. That will give you clues about your way of being in the world and how you sometimes tend to interact with some of your clients.

How the Cards and the Client or Querent Connect

Many books and websites explain the meanings of every one of the seventy-eight Tarot cards. The authors who describe them tend to be mostly consistent with each other, but some go off on their own unique tangents. When you've read a few books (including this one) you'll have a pretty good idea of meanings universally ascribed to the cards, and how they connect with each other. For the daring, this can enable a person to be on their path to becoming a reader.

Here's something to consider: Are you going to be strictly a reader of the cards, or use your cards to read people? A friend recalls, "The worst reading I ever received was from a very bright young man who knew his deck intimately. He laid down a complex spread and told me everything he imagined I'd ever need to know about the meaning of each card. I genuinely admired his deep knowledge of the cards and their diverse meanings. Too bad not much of what he said had anything to do with me."

Why? Because he left out four of the five major elements of an effective reading. These essentials are:
1. Knowledge of the cards and the structure of the deck.
2. Awareness of the querent's reactions to the cards.
3. Watching and hearing the querent's posture, gestures, movements, manner of speaking, and general attitudes.

4. Alertness to perceptions and intuitions or guesses about the querent, based on observations, sensitivities, aptitudes, and knowledge of human nature; and
5. Crafting a beneficial querent and reader relationship from the moment of initiating interaction to the conclusion of the reading.

Let's look more closely at the reading mentioned just prior. "After the young man asked if I wanted a reading and I accepted the invitation," continues the recipient, "he laid out the cards in a spread. From that moment on, he never looked up from his cards. He did not look at my facial expressions or body reactions. He did not ask how a card did or did not fit with what was happening in my life. In short, the reading was a monologue about the meanings of the cards."

II
Medicine Woman

XII
Vision Quest

Unless they are improbably brilliant, monologues can be deadly. Dialogues are often more helpful, especially when they include all five components listed here, and bear useful messages on the wings of the Tarot. Now let's examine them more closely as we return to the relationship between client and facilitator. The Native American cards remind us that the facilitator might be not just a reader or psychologist, but also a shaman, medicine woman, or grandmother, guru, or pastoral counselor.

A medicine woman, her eyes staring into the soul of her client, lets him discuss the card he has chosen, the Vision Quest.

"You know," he says, "I'm looking for something to give my life greater meaning. For me, it isn't getting rich. I make a good living. But I feel somehow empty inside."

"Perhaps you can't find what you're looking for because you don't know what it is?"

"Exactly. I'm looking for clarity and inner peace, But I don't know where or how to find them."

Their exploration continued. As he was preparing to leave, the medicine woman said,

"Of course I can't tell you where your quest will lead you. Only you can discover that. But these may help."

She thumbed through her deck and handed him three cards.

"Look carefully at these cards and memorize them. Then keep them in your mind and heart as companions and reminders."

"How is this Eight of Air, Interference, supposed to help me?"

"It is to remind you that there will always be people and situations and demands trying to pull you off your path, even after you see your vision clearly. You will feel it in your body. When you do, draw away and return to your quest. The second card, the Three of Earth, Growth, tells you to remember that discovering your quest and realizing it takes time. Diligently water the seeds you will plant, care for yourself and others, and follow your quest without fail once you know what it is. The third card, the Sun, prompts you to hold the sun in your heart. Find things to appreciate in everyone, and all beings, and in yourself."

He thanked her and left. As their encounter shows, a reading is likely to be useful only if the cards are discussed in a manner that's relevant for the person. Had the medicine woman only told him the meanings of the cards without exploring his feelings about them, he would have walked away with nothing. At some point in either a divinatory reading or a counseling session, you can invite the person to share his or her thoughts about the cards, telling how one fits or doesn't, or whether it's necessary to pick another card for clarification.

Eight of Air
Interference

Three of Earth
Growth

IXX
Sun

Also, because everyone is unique, the very same cards can have radically different meanings for different people. A central part of the reader's job is to assess *how* a given card relates to a given person. Suppose that a young woman with hunched shoulders speaks in a barely audible voice and shoots furtive glances right and left as she pulls the Major Arcana card titled Strength. In her case, discussing this card can involve looking at how she gives away her power and submits to others' wishes when she doesn't want to. It might also involve focusing on ways she could develop her potential strengths. Looking at the rest of her cards and noticing her ways of interacting with you and the images will provide clues about what those potential strengths are and what she can do to develop them.

By contrast, the next person to sit down may be confident and brash to the point of being overbearing. If he pulls the same card, it may mean that he ought to pay more attention to reducing his domineering manner that causes others to challenge him or close communications with him.

When explaining the traditional meanings of a card, its messages come alive when they are read in relation to the person's presence, (body language, voice tones, clothing style—such as a surfer or banking executive), his or her apparent emotional and relational dynamics, and way of thinking.

Also, each reader or therapist does well to draw on his or her own constellation of abilities. For example, if you're a psychic and you can close your eyes and intuitively "see" or "feel" places and events in someone's life, or if you've been trained as a nurse, and have a strong foundation of knowledge about good health and healing, you can draw on your skills to enliven your readings. Part of your task lies in assessing your own strengths and aptitudes, and intuiting or thinking about how you can use them to enrich your work.

Chances are that you are already attentive to some or all the elements of a good reading and may or may not realize it. Keeping them in mind can make your sessions more effective whether you are doing a divinatory or representational session, and whether you are working with an individual, a couple or a family.

From Accurate to Useful

An *accurate* session is one that identifies and articulates real events in a person's life and consciousness. A *useful* session is one that communicates insights in such a way that the person finds them relevant and helpful. Even if an observation is accurate, if it triggers someone's defensiveness so that he or she refuses to hear, it's not very helpful.

Just as therapists go through psychotherapy as part of their training, a reader can go to other readers to experience varied approaches to getting their cards read. Receiving readings from others provides immediate feedback about how different readers handle the cards and interact. You can also do readings for yourself and contemplate your own cards to increase your understanding. How do you use images to

Two of Water
Love

Four of Air
Contemplation

gain access into your own depths? What questions might you ask yourself that make you more reflective or receptive in the moment? Can you find new avenues of insight to guide yourself in understanding the "why," "what," or "how" of your situation and reactions? Can the Four of Air enhance and enrich your understanding of the Two of Water—or vice versa?

Your work is likely to be most effective when you allow your knowledge, intuition, and awareness of what is occurring to be totally focused in the moment on what you see, hear, and feel from the other; what's happening in you, and your sense of the relationship among you, the other person (if you are working with another), and the cards. Spontaneity is likely to naturally come into play to inspire an authentic and meaningful experience. Your table or office, however, is just one tiny bit of the other person's world.

The Field and the Life-Space

Jungian analyst James Hillman speaks of his frustration sitting in his Dallas office, spending an hour a week trying to help a client, then sending her back out into a culture that has 167 hours a week to drive her crazy. We must "re-place" the person in the world, says Hillman. "The 'bad place I am in' may refer not only to a depressed mood or an anxious state of mind; it may refer to a sealed-up office tower where I work, a set-apart suburban subdivision where I sleep, or the jammed freeway on which I commute between the two."

The first psychologist to move from taking the classical individual gestalt psychology of learning and perception into the broader spheres of personality and social life was Kurt Lewin, who taught at the University of Berlin and later in America.[1] One of his concepts was the "field." That means the physical, interpersonal, and emotional space in which a person's life takes place. Although different practitioners define the field in different ways, Lewin offered one central defining principle: "A person's interest organizes the field."

Lewin also had a more inclusive concept that he called the *life-space*. So far as we know he never explicitly defined the difference between the field and the life-space. Here is our distinction: The life-space includes all the places and people that are part of your present life, all the places where you have lived and been in the past, and even places that are part of your consciousness as a result of reading or seeing pictures or watching movies or hearing others tell stories about them. For a dedicated reader of novels, or a TV and movie buff, the vicarious life-space may be as significant as the physical one. In brief, the life-space is the entire physical and mental world within which a person's existence takes place. Of course some aspects of a person's life-space will be salient at the time of a given session and others will not. This opens the door to asking the person to select one or more cards from a face-up deck that represent elements in his or her larger life-space that limit it, expand it, or in some other way feel relevant to present concerns. Where a person's mind spends much of its time may differ from where that person's body spends most of its time.

When two college students talked about their daily physical life-spaces to each other, one chose the six of cups to describe a neat small mental map centered on her campus and the part of town near it. The other selected the knight of wands to symbolize hers, drawing long lines to represent freeways in her metropolitan area, with off-ramps and the places she frequented. The former described her life-space as mostly cheerful and upbeat while the latter's description was more threatening and alienating. The additional cards they chose as they spoke expanded those themes.

As you work with someone, you may have a sense that you want to know more about the human and physical context in which that person exists. With his or her selection of card images to represent his or her life-space, you can learn something about that person's physical and social world, and how that person perceives it. Is this person limiting their existence or opening it to new possibilities? Are most of the possibilities in it alienating or inviting? In a representational session, you might ask the person to select from a face-up deck one or more card images to reflect his or her physical neighborhood, workplace, dwelling, family, friends, physical neighborhood, and personal feelings in regard to each of these. If time is short, you can focus on the client's central interest.

A Life-Space Card Spread

For a representational session, first spread your deck face up. (In a divinatory reading, you will choose your cards from a face-down deck, but the layout is the same.) Keep your mind open to possibilities. While shifting through the different images, choose the following cards for what's happening at this moment in relation to:

ONE CARD FOR YOUR:	ONE CARD FOR YOUR FEELINGS ABOUT YOUR:
Workplace	Workplace
Dwelling or personal space	Dwelling or personal space
Family	Family
Friends or coworkers	Friends or coworkers

You can also add any other items to your spread that are important to you, or replace one of these items with another to make your personal life-space map most relevant.

• What do you see in your cards?
• Are you able to get a better sense of who you are and where your primary energy lies?
• Is there any area where you are blocked or do you find a part of your space that you want to change?

For many people, the family is the most influential aspect of their life-space. In addition, we live in an increasingly multicultural world. In the cards that illustrate this chapter, and in several other decks with Native American themes, there are no kings or queens, knights or pages, emperors or empresses. Those social roles and all that goes with them are relics of medieval and Renaissance Europe and Asia. They did not exist in most of North America. Instead, Native American decks have fathers and mothers, sons and daughters, and often a grandmother and grandfather. By extension, the sons and daughters might also be sisters and brothers. Shown here are a Mother of Air, a Father of Fire, a Son of Water, and a Daughter of Earth. The suits connect directly with the four elements symbolized by Swords, Wands, Cups, and Pentacles.

Informed by these Native American decks that reflect an egalitarian social structure not found in traditional court cards, even in divinatory readings we can ask a person whether a king might represent the person's father or a queen the mother. Might a knight or page be a sister or brother—or depending on the person's age, a son or daughter? Often the person says yes, and it can become a focus of the reading.

*Mother
of Air*

*Father
of Fire*

*Daughter
of Earth*

*Son
of Water*

Now we move from what may seem obvious on the surface to what can lie hidden in a person's depths. As we do, we will explore specific methods of using the cards in a representational way.

9 of Cups

4.

ANOTHER AVENUE: FROM DIVINATION TO REPRESENTATION

In a classical Tarot reading, after preliminary introductions and the shuffling of the cards, the querent is asked to cut the face-down cards and place them in a preselected number of stacks on the table in preparation for the reader to arrange a spread. When ready to begin the card interpretations, the reader may say something like, "Your first card represents…"

But suppose someone comes to see a counselor, therapist, or reader who uses the cards differently. The deck is spread face up on the table, and the client or querent is asked to look at the various images. Then he or she is encouraged to select cards to represent people or concerns in his or her life.

Suddenly we are in a different world. Are you willing to enter it? If you already do readings, can you suspend your familiar way of using the cards and experiment with using them in a representational manner in which the querent or client is asked to assign meanings to the card's pictures? You might begin by implementing a short representational use of the cards within your normal style of doing readings. It can be fascinating, because when using the cards in this manner, the meanings one person finds in the cards may be quite different from those someone else would see in them.

If you've been reading the cards for some time, your first reaction might be, "But it's my job to interpret card meanings. That's why people come to me for a reading." Yes, this point of view is popular and we won't argue. But for adventure and new possibilities let's look at the situation differently. Even when you give up the power of authority in relating your card interpretations, you get it back via a deeper look into the person's concerns and needs as they themselves tell you their associations to the images. The cards become a way to unmistakably hear, see, and feel something of another person's inner world. This approach asks you to suspend your outlook on the meaning of the card and instead hear the person's own statement, "This is what it means to me."

We could, of course, create a candlelit sacred ceremony of the sort that is often offered to the muses of the Tarot when beginning new work, but since we don't know whether you're a Tarot reader or psychologist, we'll pass on that. Whatever your background and expertise, we're inviting you to explore methods that use a representational approach. These involve some form of conversation about, identification with, or dialogue between images that your client has chosen to depict him or herself, and/or other images chosen to stand for another person (or people). Also, this use of images can have great value when you do this kind of reading for yourself.

With another person in a representational session, the key guideline is that you don't speak through the cards. You let the cards speak through the client or querent.

Connecting with the Cards

You might already be old friends with the Tarot, or perhaps you are recent acquaintances. In either case, at this point you'll probably find it useful to establish a relationship with the deck that you're going to use for your present explorations. This might be "Hello again" with a deck that's an old friend, "Getting to know you better" with a deck you've used just a little, or "Pleased to meet you" with a deck you've never used before.

Choosing a "Significator"

Sometimes before giving a divinatory Tarot reading, the reader will sense the energy of his or her client or querent, or talk with the person about a prominent concern, and then select a card from the seventy-eight images that feels somehow parallel to that person's energy field. Used as a visual reference point for what seems to personify their essential qualities, it will be positioned at a strategic location within the person's card spread.

We suggest that you take a few moments right now to open your deck, lay the cards face up, and silently scan through the images. Focus on those that capture your attention—for any reason. Next ask yourself, "Which card best represents me at this moment?" Choose one with imagery that seems to reflect what you're about. It might not be the same card you would have chosen yesterday or the one you might choose tomorrow. Rather, you want it to represent you at this very instant.

Choose a card now and place it in front of you. We will call it your *personal significator.* If you are keeping a Tarot journal, you might want to write this card's name in it.

Queen of Cups

Here we are imagining that you have chosen the Queen of Cups from the *Mary-El Deck*—but of course really you will make your own choice from your own deck. Look closely at your significator. Take in its details, colors, and overall impression. Ask yourself how it connects with you. For a few moments, close your eyes and in whatever way makes sense, inwardly look at it within your mind. Then, open your eyes. Breathe deeply, relax, and again look at the card for several minutes. You might begin with the line, "Now I am aware of . . ." and notice anything that occurs in your thoughts, emotions, body, spirit, and inclinations toward action. Perhaps you find that you're gritting your teeth, or tightening your calves and forearms. Maybe you feel like protecting yourself from feeling certain emotions and would rather not take time to think much about them. That's okay, too. You may even become aware of physical restraints such as the tightness of a shirt that you normally wouldn't notice. Or by contrast, you may feel warm and tingly and attracted to the card. The key is to stay in your present experience even if you think about the past or future: "Now I am aware of feeling anxious about whether my husband will like my new dress." Don't be surprised if you notice the atmosphere in your mind change dramatically when you focus on the "awareness continuum" of your moment-to-moment experience.

Have you finished? What stood out most in your reactions to this card? Do you want to take a moment to record your feelings and ideas? Is it in any way connected to your personal mythology about yourself and your world? Once you start to look, sometimes you can find worlds within worlds in a single card. In any case, keep this card face up on the table (or other surface) where you can see it.

Creating a Five-Card Personal Collage Spread

This is a spread you can use for yourself whether you're an experienced Tarot reader or therapist, or have never previously used the cards. It's useful for centering and balance, and for connecting this moment with the larger context of your present life.

Our language implies that this is a session for you yourself, but you can use these same instructions with a querent or client. Scan through the face-up deck spread out before you (minus the card you picked as a significator. While sifting through the images, choose five more cards. Pick one for each category that best relates to what's happening at this moment in your:

1. Mind
2. Emotions
3. Body (muscles, breathing, etc.)
4. Spirit
5. Primary concern or situation

Now take your five cards and lay them out in front of you in any arrangement that feels right. In Tarot reading language, you are creating a five-card collage spread. Most card layouts or spreads have specific designs and the cards are put in set positions. By contrast, in this spread you create your own unique arrangement of cards that fits the way you feel at this very moment. In the example below we've put them in a simple horizontal row, but you can put them above and below each other and sideways or at angles if you please.

Contemplate your cards for another three or four minutes. Notice every detail that stands out for you. Do any of them connect with any of your specific past or present situations? While you have your collage spread on the table, you can fill in the blanks below either in this book, your Tarot journal, or on a separate piece of paper.

From my face-up deck, I selected these cards to represent my present awareness:

ASPECT OF MYSELF	CARD CHOSEN	MY ASSOCIATIONS TO THE CARD
Mind		
Emotions		
Body		
Spirit		
Concern or situation		

Again pick up the card you chose as the significator. Place this in or above your collage spread, so that all six cards lie together before you.

A moment ago you looked at your chosen cards one at a time. Now take in your collage as a whole. Open your mind to whatever emerges from within you. Can you think of one sentence or imagine one mental picture or symbol that embodies its overall central meaning for you right now? As you continue to read this chapter, leave your collage on the table. You will need it later on pages 71 and 84.

Most Tarot readers, therapists, and counselors who use the cards in their work with others also sometimes consult the cards for themselves. The collage spread that we just described is one of many possible ways to give yourself a reading and potentially shine a new light on your situation.

Once you've selected images that portray your feelings or something else about your situation, simply look at them. Look deeply. What do they say to you? Sometimes unexpected insights emerge from our unconscious when we try to identify with the cards in this way.

Representational Uses of Imagery

When people come to you for a reading or counseling session, they may be trying to resolve an inner conflict about a future action. Or they will try to mentally or emotionally work through an issue with another person in their past or present. In either case, most often when you're working with the Tarot, you will probably be having a conversation with them about the situations, dilemmas, or conflicts depicted in selected cards. Such discussions may sometimes bring up emotional undercurrents that include memories of past traumas. The querent or client will usually have a pretty good sense of how deeply they want to go into their private inner world. Don't try to push further than is comfortable.

As you're entering the passageway into a person's deep concerns, you'll be hearing your querent or client discuss their associations to the images chosen from a deck with the cards spread out face up. You want to do your best to make sure you're hearing correctly. You may not have to do much besides ask a few questions, listen, and repeat back what you think you heard him or her say. Useful lines to deepen such a conversation may include your own variations on comments such as:

- "I think I hear you saying . . . Is that right?"
- "So your thoughts about that are . . . and you seem to feel . . . Am I hearing you accurately?"
- "I'm not sure I'm getting your meaning. Will you please say that again in different words?"
- "You seem pulled in two different directions. Can you say more about each of them?"
- "Do you really feel that way, or is someone else telling you that you ought to think or feel that way, or do that?"

Even though the range of possible responses is wide, let your intuition be your guide, and let your logic double-check what you think you're hearing. You want to be mindful of both the other person's reactions and your own in the present moment to help someone move from confusion to clarity. Learning to separate someone's own inner voices and preferences from those borrowed from others via demands or expectations is a major step.

In such a conversation, you will want to be attentive to the client's voice, gesture, postures, facial expressions, and other subtle and not-so-subtle signals. At appropriate points, such as when you see the person holding their breath, holding back tears, or tensely making a fist, you might ask, "What sensations do you experience in your body right now? Where do you sense that?" or "What are you feeling when we talk about this?"

Or you might ask about something that you seem to be hearing "between the lines." Let your intentions include helping the person develop greater ability to "be here and now" even when talking about something that's "there and then." Asking for thoughts, emotions, and body sensations in response to a card's image can be a good starting point.

Because the cards have such diverse images, they can be an excellent reference point to deepen your discussion. Whenever it feels important, you might ask your client to choose another card from the face-up deck that embodies what he or she is feeling at that moment, and then reflect on the associations that card evokes.

A concern, however, is that a person can easily end up digressing into distracting topics that avoid their main concern. While working, be alert for the tendency to digress. When it occurs, your choices include:

1. Silence;
2. Touching the cards that point to the main issue where they lie on the table;
3. Directly bringing the focus back to the issue, "You were saying that you went to your aunt's trailer and . . . "
4. A comment such as, "The issue you started out with seems difficult for you to talk about . . . is that so?"
5. Offering a choice. For example: "Do you really want to keep talking about what Lisa and Marilyn said, or would you prefer to come back to what you said was most important?"

Often you will discover that if you find your own mind wandering as the person speaks, it's probably a clue that they've moved away from what they really care about. Leave as much room for digression as you think the person needs to "catch their breath" but not more, unless they clearly show that they want to distance themselves from their central concern.

Also, sometimes a client may not pinpoint any particular issue, problem, or opportunity. In that case, after you have laid all the cards in your deck face up, let the client have a couple of minutes to choose a card that reflects an inclination, a wish, a fear, a hope, a challenge, or any other overt or hidden dimension of himself or herself that spontaneously feels important. The card might even represent a place like a home or a workplace. It can be real, or unreal but psychologically present in their mind. Discussing the images can help someone become inwardly comfortable and more willing to talk about feelings.

Perceiving Hidden Emotions

Throughout our lives, we are always meeting people. Who *is* this person you've just met—really? Or who, inwardly, is a person whom you've known for some time—but not very well? We learn about each other in various ways. Some are obvious to anyone who truly looks and listens to how people present themselves, from the expressions on their faces to the clothes they wear. There are also messages in their paralanguage— where they look, their posture, gestures, and voice tones; how close they stand to us and others, and whether they reach out to touch or hug or keep their hands rigidly by their sides. All that can be seen and heard by anyone who cares to notice. And there are patterns of behavior that are not so obvious.

Most experienced psychologists and card readers are more attentive to such clues and cues than the average person. A break in the voice or a tightening of the throat, for instance, may tell a poignant story about a person's emotional state.

Other signals are hidden. Emotions seldom travel alone. Like cards in a spread, they tend to hang out in groups. Often, however, only one item in a group is visible. For instance, a classical saying is "men get angry, women cry." But beneath the anger always lies some kind of feeling of hurt or injury. Anger is a characteristic way men respond to pain. By contrast, when a woman is hurt, beneath her tears is often anger or even rage, but our culture has taught her that it "is not ladylike" or "not nice" to show it.

Of course these are stereotypes. Some men and women respond differently. But almost always when one feeling (of whatever kind) is expressed, there is at least one more different feeling beneath it. In working with the Tarot, sometimes underlying emotions may come to the surface quickly. Or a person may need to take time to develop a sense of safety and trust before being willing to reveal their innermost feelings.

After years of watching the layers of people's emotions, we found that the cards themselves suggested a method of diving more deeply into someone's inner world. Victor coined the term "emotional stack" to refer to groups of two or more feelings lying beneath one another. Sometimes a stack contains just two feelings, and sometimes it contains a more complicated collection of emotions. A stack may contain as many as half a dozen ways of feeling mixed together. No wonder that at times people are so confused that they can't get a handle on what's going on inside themselves or another.

In social interactions, often there are at least two feelings involved in whatever statement a person makes. For example, an employee shows the boss a completed piece of work, hoping for the surface praise, "You did an excellent job on that project." But underneath may be the feelings, "I want you to like and value me as a person, and I'd love a raise." When

2 of Cups

XIII Death

you understand the principle of how we stack our emotions above and below one another, you can become more sensitive to whatever lies beneath what you see or hear on the surface.

Combinations of cards are a useful way to illustrate emotional stacks. Often we ask, "Do you have any sense of another feeling that lies beneath the one you've been describing?" We ask the person to select and lay down a card for their dominant way of feeling in a given situation. Then we suggest that they sink down into themselves to see whether they can find another way of feeling that lies beneath it (which usually they can), and then choose a card for that feeling. Or as they look through the deck, one image may trigger an underlying feeling and cause the person to feel a sudden "Yes! And I didn't even realize it." You can place the underlying card beneath the card on top so that it's partly hidden and partly visible, or ask your querent or client to do so.

The following example (with the word client sometimes also being used to represent querent) illustrates an emotional stack. A woman who is feeling anger on the surface chooses the image of the Two of Cups, illustrated with two rearing horses, to represent her feelings. She puts it on the table. When asked to find the feelings under her anger, she gets in touch with an overwhelming sense of grief for the loss of her mother who recently passed away. For that feeling she chooses the Death card. The facilitator places this card so that it is partly hidden beneath the Two of Cups.

Going Deeper into the Psyche: A Nine-Card Representational Spread That Includes Emotional Stacks

When you're ready to descend deeper into your inner world, or that of your querent or client, lay out the cards face up so that the other person (or you, if you're reading for yourself) can scan through the images. The person selects cards that complement the questions that emerge, and that help uncover feelings, memories, or inclinations that were not apparent at the start. Let's look at a real life example.

The context: In a reading, the querent/client tells the reader that she's trying to figure out how to handle a highly troubling situation with another person. The reader begins:

Card 1
Reader: "As you look through the cards, you're going to scan the images to find one that represents how you're feeling or triggers an impulse toward action that relates to the way you feel. First, choose an image to *represent the other person* in the interaction you're concerned about—one

that shows how he or she usually acts toward you in such situations. After you've picked a suitable card, place it face up on the table."

Client: The woman chooses the major card, The Devil, and places it in the middle of the table, near the reader.

Reader: "It looks like you're unhappy with someone. Who?"

Client: "It's my boyfriend. That SOB! I really hate him right now. He's like a devil to me."

Card 2
Reader: "Look through the cards again, and choose an image to *represent yourself—one that shows how you see yourself being with him*. Place this card about six inches above Card One."

Client: Client chooses the Ten of Wands.

Reader: "How does this card make you feel?"

Client: "Angry and depressed. I keep looking down at what's been spilled out of my heart and I feel so insecure and emotionally drained."

Reader: "Do you want to tell me what's happened to make you feel this way?"

Client: "My boyfriend who lives with me slept with my best friend when I went to work. Now I hate them both and I can't stand to be with him. I feel so violated."

Card 3
Reader: "Can you find a picture that shows a feeling or impulse that underlies the emotion reflected in the Ten of Wands, one that shows what you're feeling or expressing that is hidden under the surface?"

Client: Client chooses the Queen of Disks.

Reader: "What do you see in this card?"

XIX The Sun
X The Wheel of Fortune
Queen of Disks
10 of Wands

Client: "I have tears running out of one eye and down my cheek and I look stricken with grief and can't see out of the other eye so I can't see anything clearly. I want to scream and I can't. I want to hold on to something, but I know love isn't real and I'm only going to get more beaten down." The reader slips this card partway under Card Two to create an emotional stack.

6 of Swords
Knight of Swords
Knight of Cups
XV The Devil

Reader: "You have to be brave to face such painful emotions. Betrayal by a lover is a valid reason to be upset and angry. Are you okay looking for another card that expresses more about what you're feeling?"

Client: "No! I want to scream and not look at cards."

Reader: "Okay. No one is nearby, so if you want to scream, go ahead, scream."

Client: Starts to cry and looks away.

Reader: "Here's a tissue. You have my total support for what you're feeling. Love can be painful as well as wonderful." Reader goes into silence and let's the woman have a few moments to cry.

Card 4
Reader: "When you're ready, let's look at the cards again. I see your pain, and I'm sorry you're hurting, but it can be healing when you give yourself permission to talk about emotions. Can you focus on the cards once more?"

Client: "I . . . I think so."

Reader: "Look for a card that shows what feelings you think underlies the message conveyed by The Devil, the first card you choose?"

Client: "My best guess is this card: The Wheel of Fortune."

Reader: "What does this card have to do with The Devil?"

Client: "Just like that figure in the boat, I'm going to be leaving. I'm going to get myself away from The Devil and his lies."

Reader: "You have to find a way to reclaim your balance to handle a situation like this. Are you strong enough to face The Devil and tell him what you're thinking?"

Client: "I see myself going away forever. My boyfriend doesn't get my love anymore and I'm changing the locks on my door so he can't get into our home."

Reader: Takes the Wheel of Fortune card and slips it partway under the Queen of Disks. "Is that what you want to do?"

Client: "I don't know what I want to do! I haven't talked with my boyfriend since we had our blow-out."

Card 5
Reader: "The following might be a bit tricky, but if you imagine that the other person has more than one feeling or impulse that underlies his way of acting or speaking toward you, choose a card that shows *your best guess* about what it is."

Suspicions, Guesses, Projections, and Hypotheses

Where we've used and italicized the words "your best guess" in the prior text, it's a reminder that even a querent or client who thinks they're keenly logical or intuitive is still *projecting* his or her own thoughts and feelings on to the other person. Your client is offering *hypotheses* about the other's inner world. In other words, they're guessing. They may be right, wrong, or partly right. Similarly, if feasible, when you have hypotheses, guesses, or suspicions about what's going on inside the mind of someone else, check them out. It's better to be right than just think you're right—even if the reality is different from what you want to hear.

Client: After looking through the cards, she chooses the Knight of Cups. "I know he loves me and wants to be with me. We talk about having children and a family together. But he's just destroyed my trust. How can I believe him?"

Reader: "Right now you don't have to make any final decisions about what to do. You wouldn't be crying if you didn't care about him and your relationship. In any case, you're going to need to communicate with him if you're living together. Perhaps you'll feel better when you can ask him questions about your life together. Because you've chosen a card that shows a flower and gentleness, maybe there's more hope than hopelessness in your situation."

Card 6 and 7

Reader: "Now, choose a card that represents the way you would like the other person to speak, act, and be with you, or your guess about how he or she wants to be with you but doesn't know how to."

The Fool

Client: Chooses The Knight of Swords and Six of Swords.

Reader: "What do these images mean to you?"

Client: "Tom always wants to be right and he has to be in charge. His ego puts a crown on his head even when he's wrong, like the man riding the owl in this picture."

Reader: "Is he willing to give and take feedback when you have disagreements?"

Client: "Let me just say that he isn't always agreeable."

Reader: Places The Knight of Swords a few inches under the Knight of Cups, partly visible. "Do you want to say more about that?"

Client: "He always wants to be dominant. He can be annoying, but he's a really good lover in many ways, especially in the bedroom. And I love his love!"

Reader: "That last comment sounds like it's connected with conflicting ideas about what you want, with trying to cut through difficult feelings, and with this Six of Swords." (Reader slips the card beneath the others in Tom's stack.)

Card 8

Reader: "Now choose a card to represent how you would like to speak, act, and be with your boyfriend, even if you don't know how, or don't feel strong enough or free enough to do so."

Client: Chooses Major Arcana, The Sun.

Reader: "Sun energy is light and positive. Do you want to tell me why you chose this card?"

Client: "I always feel good when I sit in the sun. I want to feel emotional warmth and I want to trust." (Reader places this card in the stack that represents the client.)

Reader: "Now lets look at the 'I want' or 'I need' statements between yourself and Tom. Is there any chance that either of you may be willing to provide what the other wants?"

Client: After the client finished contemplating the cards, she shrugged her shoulders and said, "I don't know!"

Card 9

Reader: "Okay. Please scan through the face-up deck and find one card that points to how you envision yourself talking in forthcoming interactions with Tom.

Client: Chooses The Fool.

Reader: Holds the card so that the image is visible above remaining cards in the spread and says: "What's happening in your mind?"

Client: "Can't you tell? I'm feeling foolish for being in love with a cheater, a fool for being fooled in love. I'm struggling to not feel like the fool, but I am a fool and very confused!"

Reader: "The Fool takes many forms. It may indeed mean someone who is foolish. Or in medieval times the outfit was often a disguise for a king's secret advisor. Or the fool may be everyman or everywoman trying to find out what's really happening without expectations or distortions. Does this last meaning work for you? You don't know whether that night meant your connection is collapsing or whether it was a young man's one-night fling and you may yet work out a deeply loving relationship. You can try to release your 'foolish' notions and use your full awareness to be a wise woman as you move ahead."

Client: "Well, that gives me a lot to think about. Can I draw The Star? That's a beautiful card."

In the prior example, for the most part the client chose cards with no thought about their traditional divinatory meanings. She was responding almost entirely to the pictures on the cards and what they evoked in her.

Revisiting Your Collage

Now that you've seen a demonstration of using emotional stacks, would you like to try it yourself? It's a good time to experience this process. Hopefully, you still have your collage spread nearby. Look back now at the personal collage spread you previously created and set aside.

From the cards you selected to represent different aspects of yourself, choose one from the category mind, emotions, body, or spirit. The card that has the most significance for you is a good choice. Once you've made your selection, continue reading.

How do you feel about this card? Now, hold that thought and think about what feelings might lie beneath its surface. What comes to mind? From your face-up deck select and lay down a card that represents the first underlying feeling you become aware of. Slide it partially under the card in your collage that you designated as "having the most significance."

Adding this card points to a deeper aspect of what's occurring within you. Also, you have just created a two-card emotional stack. If you become aware of yet another feeling as you do this, you can add a third card, again placing it beneath the others with enough of it visible to show what it is. What you are doing is allowing images on the cards to help you discover and communicate with your deeper feelings.

News from the Body

At first glance, somatic reactions, such as tension, relaxation, and gestures or posture, may seem to be generally connected with emotions. With further investigation, you may discover that some tensions are located in particular places in the body for a reason. One person may hold tension in her forehead, or her jaw, another in his fists, another in his calves or feet. Tensions in these different areas may be related to different psychological reactions, such as holding back fear or biting back an impulse toward aggression. Similarly, shoulders hunched in a protective manner usually reflect something quite different than a forward-thrusting chin. A hand that makes a chopping motion into the other palm may suggest the very opposite of weakly upturned palms and shrugging shoulders. Such actions and reactions often visibly display our emotions.

Sometimes the difference between a card reading and counseling is a distinctly different way of proceeding. Sometimes it is a difference of degree. But however you are conducting your session, noticing and understanding this nonverbal information can help you better understand a person.

We have just looked at methods of using the cards for self-inquiry and discovering hidden feelings. In Chapter 5, we will review these methods and add additional depth to help us understand invisible strata of concern.

2 of FIRES

PART II

Representational Uses of the Cards

ACE of CUPS

5.

CONNECTING THE SURFACE AND THE DEPTHS

"Going where no one has gone before . . ." So begins the narration for the later episodes of *Star Trek*, the most widely watched science fiction series of the twentieth century. It explores the excitement of strange worlds, uncharted civilizations, and even the dynamic dance of light and shadows in the human mind. In the absence of a ticket for a spaceship ride, our present adventure leads us to an inward passage that can open doors to spectacular vistas of consciousness. Here we see how a counselor, psychotherapist, coach, reader, or even a meditation teacher can guide a person on a journey into interior worlds of the self, with the hope of emerging more personally aware and more effective in the world.

As we saw previously, "stacks" of two or more cards can expand our awareness of what's going on with a person and their life situation. With that as our starting point, here we more fully explore the use of stacks, and go on to show how to combine Tarot and other visual images with methods from gestalt therapy, and psychodrama, and other approaches used in counseling and therapy.

Some of this material summarizes what we have already discussed. We seek to provide an opportunity for you to review our process step by step with ample time to follow our procedures and practice the material. Then in the chapters that follow, we will move into new territory.

Taking Emotional Stacks to the Next Level

For clarity, first we explicitly describe each step in the process of using emotional stacks. As you've seen, by adding another card—or in some cases even two cards or several—we increase the potential to go deeper into the internal dynamics of a perplexing or emotionally charged situation. (Note: Our suggested card order will not always be most appropriate. Be flexible with card arrangements in relation to the demands of your situation.)

In a reading, sometimes a client will hide their true feelings because they feel guilty or assume that you will judge them as a bad person because of their problem or situation. Doing an emotional stack as part of your readings enables a person to tiptoe inward for the purpose of self-discovery, reducing the fear of too much self-disclosure. Also, if your client is having some kind of trouble with another person, or relationship problems that you guess may be rooted to one or more traumatic past situations, you might suggest using the cards to explore their inner process. If your client says yes to this idea, spread your deck of imagery-rich cards face up on your table or whatever surface is accessible and have the person select their first card.

Sometimes your client may choose several cards to symbolize different people. When that occurs, during the initial comments that reveal who or what the cards represent, you will probably see, hear, or sense clues telling you which card(s) has the dominant charge of energy.

If your client is familiar with the Tarot, you might say something like, "Don't think about the cards' traditional meanings. For right now, choose only cards with images that connect with your feelings or noteworthy associations."

Steps in a "Beneath the Surface" Card Spread

Each of us has a story to tell about something we care about. Every story is a narrative that we have woven, or perhaps borrowed from another. We constantly maintain them through the statements we make to ourselves and others, and the pictures or mind-movies we show and play on our inner mental screens. The methods described here help the therapist, counselor, or card reader discover those stories. They also help a person become aware of what they themselves do that contributes to those stories. That may make it possible to choose to do something else instead. Often enough, such a "something else" opens up a spectrum of new possibilities.

In the following step-by-step example of this working process coming up, in which we posit that the cards were drawn intentionally from a face-up deck, we invite you to imagine the person's situation, their actions, and their inner world, based solely on the images. We show and describe the cards but purposely do not say what they represent for the client or querent. We offer no explanations, no interpretations. Just take note of the meanings you yourself find in this demonstration spread.

Card 1. *The Other.*

Have your client choose a card to represent the other person in their present external situation. This card should include an image that typifies how he or she usually acts toward the client. If the person with whom your client has their issue is dead or has disappeared from their life, place the card sideways on the table. This placement is a reminder that you might have to work through grief or other feelings involving loss or a lost opportunity. A card might also represent something inanimate, such as a company or agency where the person works, has worked, or was fired. For this example, we will imagine that the client has chosen the Knight of Swords, who in this deck appears as a powerful, even overwhelming figure.

Card 2. *The Self.*

Secondly, have your client choose a card that represents him or herself, especially how he or she feels when interacting with the "other." For instance, your client might choose the Five of Cups, which shows an emotional interference or lack of ability to communicate with the other. Since this card shows both a man and woman, the client can identify with either.

Card 3. *Underlying emotion.*

Next have the client choose a card that shows a feeling or impulse that underlies the emotion and actions represented by Card 2. Slip it partway under Card 2. Here the Three of Swords is chosen.

Card 4. *Another underlying feeling toward the other.*

Let's assume that the person has more than one underlying feeling or impulse toward "the other." Have him or her choose a card for that additional feeling and slip it partway under Cards 2 and 3. The Two of Swords is selected.

At this point, in a single image that includes the three cards just mentioned in an almost-open stack, we have a picture of the client's dominant feelings in this situation, and another single card that tells us something about the other person who plays a leading role in this reading or therapy session. Now we turn our attention back to that other person

Card 5. *Client's guess about the other.*

Have your client choose a card that shows his or her best guess about a feeling or impulse underlying the surface emotion of the other person represented by the Card 1. Slip it partway under Card 1. Here the client chooses the Ten of Swords to represent what is imagined to be the other's underlying feeling.

Card 6. (USE ONLY IF APPLICABLE).
Client's guess about a yet deeper feeling in the other.

If your client imagines that the other person has more than one kind of feeling or impulse that underlies his or her usual way of acting or speaking toward him or herself, have your person choose a card that shows his or her best guess about what it is, and slip it under Card 5. Here the Three of Wands is chosen.

"Beneath the Surface" Emotional Stack Spread II

At this point we see the client's personal emotional stack and have a visual representation of what he or she imagines to be the other person's hidden feelings, thoughts, and or inclinations.

Using the emotional card stacks as a starting point, ask the client to discuss the kind of interaction that occurs between him or herself and the other person. This includes discussion of the known or imagined underlying feelings being represented in Cards 3, 4, 5, and 6 that affect the relationship. If this talk triggers other thoughts or feelings not shown in the stacks, it's okay. When this discussion comes to a suitable stopping point, go on to Card 7.

Card 7. *The ideal other.*

Have the client choose a card that shows the way he or she would like the other person to speak, act, and be in their encounters. Place this card a few inches above the card stack the client created to represent the other person. In this example the Nine of Cups is selected.

Card 8. *The ideal self.*

Have the client choose a card to represent how he or she would like to speak, act, and be with the other person (and perhaps doesn't know how or feel strong enough to do). Place Card 8 a few inches above the card stack the client has created to reflect him- or herself. In this example the Two of Cups is chosen.

Ideal Interaction Spread

Now look back over the entire spread of cards that symbolizes both your querent or client and/or the other person. Think about what the cards seem to say about the relationship (and also about what they don't seem to say). Then ask the client to think about the kind of interaction that he or she would like to occur. What are the "I want" or "I need" statements from the client? What does your client imagine are the "I want" or "I need" statements from the other person? How might he or she find out whether there is any chance that either of them would be willing to provide what the other wants?

Card 9. *Potential resolution.*

After the client is finished reacting to the cards, you can ask him or her to scan through the face-up deck and find one card that points to a

potential resolution or positive direction that he or she can envision. This might involve working out some kind of change in an interaction pattern with the other person, or it might involve personal inner work to change something in the client's own way of being with the other. Here the Three of Pentacles is chosen.

Finally, let all the cards that have been chosen make up a single composite image. To the left is the Other's emotional stack, with "what is wanted from the other" next to it. To the right is the person's own emotional stack, with "what is wanted" above it. Finally, centered above all the cards for both people is the "potential resolution" card. In a real reading or counseling session, it may be useful for the person to take a picture of the whole spread and later, take it out and reflect on it. Here's how it looks.

Exploring Feelings: Doing
Your Own Three-Card Emotional Stack

Before using this method with another person, it's best to try it for
yourself so that you can experiment with looking at images in relation

to your own thoughts and emotions. For a minute or two, close your eyes and go inward. Remember a relatively recent emotion provoking situation you've experienced. Look at it with your mind's inner eye. Hear the words that were spoken (if there were any) with your mind's inner ear. Be sensitive to any sensations (such as shallow breathing or tense shoulders) in your body and any inclinations toward action (such as punching someone or begging their forgiveness) that you may have felt. Then open your eyes and select three cards from your face-up deck, one for each of your three most significant feelings related to that situation. Choose them in the following order:

First, pick a card with images that represent your dominant *present here-and-now feeling* as you recall the situation.

Then scan for a "right now" feeling *that underlies your dominant emotion* and find a card that you can associate with it. Explore your awareness and feelings that go with it, as you experience it again right now. Place the second card so that it is partly covered by the first card you chose.

Next, "sink down deeper." Can you find yet another feeling hidden beneath those two? Is there some feeling or inclination that you're ignoring because it's easier not to look at or experience it? Choose a card for this feeling and slide it somewhat under the partly visible second card.

Show the three partially overlapping cards in their proper order, with the most obvious feeling on top, the one underlying that beneath it, and one representing the least visible emotion on the bottom. The least visible one may or may not be the weakest or least important. Now reflect for a moment on the entire stack: What stands out to you? If you like, you can write down the answer to these questions, either on this page or a separate piece of paper.

✎ My primary focus when pulling these cards has been:

_____

_____

_____

_____

▱▷ My dominant feeling about this situation is . . .

_____
_____
_____
_____

▱▷ The card I chose to represent the feeling associated with this situation is. . .

_____
_____
_____
_____

▱▷ As I scanned the cards to help understand my deeper emotional response, the next feeling I discovered was . . .

_____
_____
_____
_____

▱▷ The card I chose to represent this underlying feeling is . . .

_____
_____
_____
_____

▱▷ My most hidden feeling about this situation and the card I chose to represent it is . . .

_____
_____
_____
_____

There may be even more emotions mixed up in your situation, but here we're creating a three-card stack. These cards can make it easier for you to reflect on your situation and give you plenty to think about. But, if you want to descend to a deeper level and feel comfortable choosing another card(s) to help you do so, go ahead. If not, don't.

Now reflect on your card choices. Have you discovered anything new? Do you have more clarity?

If you'd like to reduce the emotional charge on the situation represented in your stack, you can consciously relax, close your eyes, and imagine your situation or unresolved event moving toward a resolution. Keep looking through your mind's eye and envision positive potentials that your heart can gladly embrace. Let them run through your mind like a movie from start to finish over and over again. As you do, be alert to notice when you are feeling anxious or tensing up physically anywhere in your body, and each time you do so, release this stress by sensing it leaving your body with your out-going breath. This method can also be helpful to help clients relax. But if someone is extremely agitated, it may not be easy to let go of a difficult memory, even when you are asking someone to think of positive potentials. In that case, rather than insisting that the person do this visualization process, you might go through a full-body relaxation sequence, and then return to normal everyday awareness.

A Further Consideration

If you still have available your collage spread that you created in the previous chapter, you can think about it in relation to the emotional card stack you just created. Is your stack related to one or more of the collage cards, or does it stand independently on its own? If it's connected with your collage spread, which card(s) is it connected with? Is there any message for you in looking at these two spreads in relation to one another?

In counseling or psychotherapy, identifying an emotional stack may be only the beginning of deeper explorations. These may occur through discussion or enactment and dialogues, as described in the very next chapter and in Chapters 7, "Inner Dialogues," and Chapter 8, "Multiple Others." When doing short Tarot readings, *identifying a stack but going no further* may be the best course of action. It is remarkable how much clarity can emerge from doing no more than identifying the emotions that are mixed up together in a situation. Ten or fifteen minutes are often enough to do that. With this method, initially the weighty feelings shown in the lower cards may be hidden. Even the client may be unaware of them. When they come to light, opaque or mixed-up feelings can become transparent.

Sometimes you may prefer to get a fuller sense of what's going on within a person before using the cards to go into his or her issue more deeply. Or you may get signals from the client that he or she prefers to move slowly, and does not want to dive into verbalizing as yet unspoken feelings. The person may prefer to stay in the womb of his or her innermost being and be suckled drop by drop with your coaching. In this case, after the initial "statement from" each card, you can take a minute or a few to explore what each of the energetically charged cards has to say as related by your client's impressions. What issues do they represent? When and if the inner conflict becomes easier to discuss, and a fuller context is established, you can move into an exploratory dialogue between the cards in a stack to help further understanding of the situation. In Chapter 6 we describe a means to carry out such a dialogue. In the approach described, you are putting the client at ease by "nibbling around the edges" before moving into big issues.

Never force your client (or yourself) to go where he or she doesn't want to go. Use a method that works for this particular person and his or her situation rather than being committed to a given method if it doesn't feel right. Also, use an approach that makes you want to move forward rather than one with which you feel uncomfortable.

What some people need most is an impartial, sensitive listener who offers them a container to hold their feelings. We know one young man who went to a counselor for six months and when we asked what went on there, he replied, "Pretty much I just talk and she listens. She doesn't say much. But I don't have anyone else who I can tell all my problems to, and I'm feeling better, clearer, and less confused." Similarly using the cards to establish a connection with someone that leads to feeling better about one's self is a valuable objective.

Now, however, we will describe more active approaches to helping people work through their conflicts and better understand their emotions. If you're ready it's time to turn the page.

6.

—

FROM DISCOVERY TO REBIRTH: IDENTIFICATION, ENACTMENT, AND PROJECTIVE DIALOGUES

TWO OF SWORDS

Images on Tarot cards are excellent starting points for telling a story about something in a person's life. Even though stories usually are told in words, a person can animate their tale with gestures to enliven it and show how she or he is being affected. This approach involves using the cards as signs that point to memories or to experience what lies hidden in their psyches. In this approach no predictions are made, and the cards are not used to tell a person what his or her problem is.

Identifying with images on cards allows people to interact with others who live within their psyche even when they are no longer in the person's daily life. It also makes it possible to actually experience different sides of the self, rather than just talking about them. Using such card work during therapy has the advantage of directly engaging troublesome feelings and inner voices that are typically kept at a distance, so that they can be addressed and resolved. Also, the methods of projective identification and role-enactment described below allow someone to enact —that is, act out— old memories in the present like an actor on a stage.

These healing processes make it possible to hear the arguments between conflicting inner voices more clearly than usual—voices that keep rising to the surface or taunting from the back of the mind. When you use these methods, while you, or you and another person, are dealing with a past event that is still causing pain in the present, you can explore it as if it is happening right now. You can become aware at this very moment of the feelings, thoughts, physical, and behavioral dimensions of it that usually lurk in the shadows of your mind and body. Those who already use art therapy, play therapy, a sand tray, or psychodrama are likely to be able to slide seamlessly into working similarly with cards. For others it may take more practice.

Before doing this type of card work with a client, it's best to experience it with another person who is also learning these methods (or a friend who is not learning them)—or even with several different people. If possible, one person will first take the role of facilitator and the other of client or querent. When you've finished such a session, you can reverse roles.

For some people, however, the following methods of the projective identification and role-enactment we describe are not a good fit. Even in deep therapeutic interactions where such exploration could be useful, a conversational style will suit them better. For others, these methods may work wonders. Inquiry will help you determine if your client is open to such work or not.

Identification and Projective Dialogues

We have explored using the cards to show how one or even several feelings can hide beneath an emotion that shows on the surface. Now we move into active *identification* with cards that you or your client or querent select during a session. This involves asking a person to identify with the central image on the card, or even with just one or two of the less prominent symbols on it. The person doesn't have to understand a card's conceptual groundings, but has to identify with it and react emotionally on some level in order to feel what that image personally embodies for him or her.

In this process, after the client selects two cards, usually from a face-up deck, instead of the facilitator having a discussion with the client, the latter is asked to identify with the images, and while identifying with each of them, express their feelings or concerns. As previously mentioned, some might feel fine with identification but not with a dialogue between the images (or different parts of their inner self). Select an approach that fits the energy and willingness of your client. You can suggest the possibility of such a dialogue, and they can accept the suggestion or not.

Note that while such Tarot work is suitable for therapy and counseling, many card reading venues are not suitable environments for this approach. In most cases privacy is paramount for a person to be willing to do such work.

Step by step, the process described here sometimes has elements in common with the exploration of emotional stacks described previously, but with major differences in method. For convenience, in the description that follows we will assume that you are the client, or are doing a reading for yourself and choosing your cards from your face-up deck.

Working with Identification

The Three-Card Self-Discovery Spread
You or your client or querent will pull three cards and lay them horizontally on the table. Suppose for the moment that you are the client or querent.

Card 1:
Begin by choosing the card that feels *most relevant to you as a person or to your question or situation*. Take a minute or two (or even a few) to imagine that you are that card. Scrutinize it carefully. Let the card's image become a springboard for deepening your understanding of your feelings in the matter of concern. First, what overall impressions and responses do you have? Then look more closely and notice each detail. Without using the card's title, describe yourself as the card image. For example, "I am standing by a table alone, wearing fancy clothes, with five cups that have been knocked over and their contents spilled out on the ground. I feel lost . . . , I think. . . , I want to . . . " Don't leave any reactions out. If you're doing your own reading, you can say these things either silently or out loud to yourself. If you're working with another person, it's good to imagine that you're one card speaking to another of the cards and share your dialogue out loud.

Card 2:
Next, in relation to your situation, *choose a card for a person with whom you often interact in the present, or with whom you interacted in the past.*

In this process, this is the person you identify as the "Other." If Card 1 turned out to represent this same person in your life rather than yourself, you can continue here with that card or choose another card that portrays that same person, or you might want to choose a card to portray a different person. This might be your father, mother, sibling, boss, or even an enemy. As you did with the first card, really "get into being" the image and identify as fully as possible with the other person. As you imagine what goes on in the mind and emotions of that other person represented in the card, "become" the other as fully as you can. Describe how you feel, sense, and think about yourself. Finish sentences he or she would speak such as, "I like. . . I want. . . I have . . . I don't have. . . I'm afraid of . . . I'm worried that. . . I look forward to . . . I anticipate . . . I expect, . . . I hope. . ." Just a few words or a phrase can finish any of those sentences. Because you want to move into feelings rather than intellectualize about them, reply quickly. (If you're working with a client and they have to take time to "think about it," you may want to skip the items that they have to mull over.) You don't have to answer all the questions—just any for which something comes right to mind. Can you imagine what it feels like to "walk in his or her shoes?" Also, consider whether the card imagery itself suggests any unexpected insights into the character or behavior of the person you chose it to represent.

Card 3:
Now *choose a card to* represent *yourself as you speak and act and feel in your interactions with that other person.* Notice your tone of voice, your posture, your movements and mannerisms as you feel yourself identifying with the card image you chose. Get as clear a sense as you can of the inner and outer details of your behavior with the other person and/or the image you chose. Then ask yourself, "Do these identifications with the Other, and with myself as I am with the Other, offer me any awareness or insight that I didn't already realize, or that I prefer not to notice?"

Enactment and Movement

If you used postures, gestures, and/or voice tones to fit the feelings described in relation to chosen cards, you have already experienced card enactment. *Ham it up—amp it up!* Stand and move as if you are that card's image or person, if you're not already doing so. Sense whether, and if so, how you are moving differently from your usual movement habits. Then *exaggerate* what's different in the way you're moving as you enact the card. Continue whatever you're doing, but do it more intensely in relation to the most noteworthy images, and whatever sensations emerge. Does any new insight, awareness, or feeling come up?

Working with Projective Dialogue to Go One Step Further

With two cards, just as you did in the Self-Discovery Spread (such as the card for yourself and one for the other person), first continue to feel your way into identifying with each of them as you've already done. Or if you prefer to select and explore two different cards, go ahead. Then begin an explicit make-believe dialogue between the two cards, or the two people represented by the cards if indeed they represent two people, one of whom might or might not be you. Focus on your central concern if there is one. Emphasize whatever the pictures on the cards mean to you. Because feelings are subjective, don't worry about validation for being right or wrong. Become the voice for one card image and the associations it triggers in you, and say whatever you like to the person or circumstance represented by the other card.

Next reverse roles: become the voice of the other card and reply. (When you are facilitating this process for a client you will offer guidance about when to switch back and forth from one role to the other.) Continue the back-and-forth dialogue for as long as needed to communicate everything that seems to matter.

Then look at those same cards once more. Now if you haven't already done so, look not just *at* the card, but look *through* it and visualize the person it represents. Also notice any relevant behavior that you didn't bring in when you identified with the card that you previously chose to depict yourself. If anything vital has been left unsaid or undone, say or do it now—concisely, strongly, graciously, or in whatever manner seems to fit.

Let's review this progression. After you (or your client) select at least two emotionally significant cards, assess where the central energy lies, and if appropriate, focus on what is being triggered. Alternatively, you can "wade in slowly," starting with cards that are on the periphery of the issue and then gradually moving to what's most central. If the two cards represent real people in your present or past life, or you and another person, first identify with the card, and then if you're willing, let yourself slide into "being" the people they represent, with their real ways of acting in the world. Then begin the dialogue, going back and forth as you speak for each card in turn. Surprising and valuable insights can emerge from unrehearsed dialogues between cards that may have much to say to each other.

If by chance the cards you're using now are not the same ones you used in the "Identification" and "Enactment and Movement" sections above, you may find yourself acting in different roles. What's important here is experiencing this process and gaining information to help you understand your situation better and become more aware, moment-by-moment, of what you actually do in it.

The Working Process in a Live Session

Now let's put aside the "How to" groundwork and move to a real example describing a process used in a psychotherapy session. It includes four elements we have described: emotional stacks, identification, enactment, and projective dialogue.

Lillian has been telling her therapist that she feels depressed and powerless. At one point the therapist asks whether she'd be willing to browse through a deck of pictorial images to see whether any reflect the way she feels. Lillian says okay, and the therapist spreads the deck face up before her. Immediately Lillian perks up just a bit, intrigued by all the images.

"Don't worry about the titles and numbers on the cards," says Natalie, the therapist. "Just notice which images call out to you. First look for a card that reflects the feelings you've been telling me about."

Lillian thumbs through the cards and chooses the Nine of Swords, which shows a woman who appears to be in despair. (She is reacting to the image. No one has offered any interpretation of what the card means, and she has no experience with the Tarot.)

Lillian: "This is how I feel. Life is hopeless and I see nowhere to go."

Natalie: "Okay. Now see if you can find a picture that might shine some light on why you feel so discouraged, or how you experience that feeling."

Lillian: "Here, this one shows it perfectly." She holds up the Eight of Swords. "I feel just like her—all tied up. With whatever I want to do, something is stopping me and I can't move ahead. And I've no idea how to get out of feeling this way."

Natalie: "Go into your body. Find the places you sense are connected with those thoughts and feelings and tell me what you find."

Lillian: (Pauses for about two minutes, then speaks.) "It's as if it hurts to breathe. I feel like I shouldn't move my arms, but just my hands. Like the tin man on his journey to Oz, my neck is tight, but it keeps me from looking at something that I'm afraid I shouldn't see. I feel slightly tense all over, especially in my shoulders."

Natalie: "It sounds like you're really stressed. As we go on, continue to sense what's occurring anywhere in your body and tell me about it immediately—no matter whatever else you're thinking and feeling. Now stand up like the woman in the picture, move around the room, and tell me what else you sense and feel."

Lillian stands up and walks in a slow circle.

Lillian: "I feel immobilized, like it's hard to do even this. Something seems to be holding me back."

Natalie: "Exaggerate that movement and tell me what you feel as you do."

Lillian walks even more stiffly and slowly and feels her arms and legs tighten.

Lillian: "It feels like someone heavy is sitting on my shoulders and holding my arms against my body with his legs."

Natalie: "Find just one sound or word or phrase that reflects what you feel and say it over and over as you walk."

Lillian *(instantly)*: "Get off my back!"

Natalie: "Good. Continue."

Lillian: "*Get off my back*. . . Get off my back. . . GET OFF MY BACK!"

Natalie *(after a minute or two)*: "Okay, that's enough." She slips the Eight of Swords part way under the Nine of Swords so that both are visible. "Now look through the cards again and see if you find one that reflects any other feeling that underlies these two."

Lillian: After a minute of moving cards around she points to one that shows a man wearing a crown and holding a sword. "This one." (The King of Swords)

Natalie: "What meaning does it have for you?"

Lillian: "It's heavy masculine power. He's pushing me down with the point of his sword and keeping me under his control. I'm only allowed to say and do what he wants me to. He doesn't let me to do anything on my own. I feel a knot in my stomach."

Natalie: "Good. Now this might be uncomfortable, but I want you to let go of being Lillian—shake your body a few times to loosen up if you like—and then feel yourself to be like the man in that picture as fully as you can. Try to *become* him."

Lillian feels slightly nauseous as she looks at the picture, but complies, feeling a little better as she shakes her arms and shoulders.

Natalie: "Now, stand as he would stand. Speak as he would speak. Move and gesture as he might do. And tell Lillian what she may and may not do."

Lillian: She draws herself up. Her face tightens. Her voice grows loud and strong. "YOU WILL DO ONLY WHAT I TELL YOU. DO YOU UNDERSTAND?"

Natalie: "Does he remind you of anyone?"

Lillian: "Mm. . . my. . . my father and uncle and grandpa all rolled into one."

They have found the root of her depression. She is not allowed to be herself. Voices she carries inside herself all the time tell her she is not allowed to be adventurous or have any freedom in her life.

At this point, Natalie senses that Lillian is ready to move from becoming aware of the roots of her conflict to taking a step toward moving out of it. She is ready to move from discovery and awareness into finding new ways to be that will replace her father's internalized demands that constantly hold her down.

Natalie: "All right. Now find a card that shows what you would like to tell the three controlling men in your family."

Lillian pulls out a card that shows a woman and a lion together with an infinity symbol above her head titled Strength.

Lillian: "I want to be like this. I want to talk back and tell them all to *shut the fuck up and back off.*"

Natalie: "Go ahead." She moves the Strength card a few inches away from the spread that contains the previously chosen cards. "In your mind, become that woman in the card who is strong enough within herself to tame that great lion." Stand up and move like her. Talk back!"

Lillian stands and breathes deeply, but her words come out small and quiet.

Lillian: "It's not fair. You have no right to make me do everything your way. I have a right to be myself." Her voice sounds like it's coming from a six-year old child.

Natalie: "Again, exaggerate the tiny, quiet childlike quality in your voice."

Lillian does so. She is able to hear herself.

Lillian: "Wow—I had no idea."

Natalie: "Now do the opposite. Remember your posture and stand tall. Take a deep breath. Stretch your arms outward and speak louder."

Lillian *(standing taller)*: "It's not fair. I have a right to be myself." Her throat opens enough to speak a little more loudly.

Natalie: "Yet again. Make a sweeping gesture with your entire arms. And this time SHOUT at him. Say the same thing over again several times." (Natalie's voice has risen in order to model speaking more loudly, so that she herself is almost shouting.)

Lillian: "I HAVE A RIGHT TO BE MYSELF!" Some of the power from the voice of the King of Swords is creeping into Lillian's own lion-tamer self. "I HAVE A RIGHT TO BE MYSELF! I DON'T HAVE TO BE HOW YOU WANT ME TO. I CAN BE ME!!!"

Then she exhales and starts to make growling sounds. Natalie asks Lillian to resume the dialogue, with The King and the Strength cards each saying just a line or two back and forth to each other. Lillian complies with short, brisk statements. After about two minutes Natalie senses that Lillian had enough of that process.

Natalie: "Wonderful. Are you willing to take one more step? Look for another picture that shows someone just as strong as the woman with the lion, but that better reflects the way you yourself would like to be strong."

After some delay Lillian picks a card titled The Star that shows a naked woman pouring water from a pitcher into a pond and a star in the sky behind her.

Lillian: "This is what I want—to be close to the earth. I want to truly be me in a gentle, graceful way that feels like who I am deep down inside."

Natalie places The Star card part way on top of the Strength card, so that the latter is still visible.

Natalie: "This is your true self that you are getting more in touch with. Are there any other dimensions to it that you're aware of?"

They continue discussing the Star image for a time, with Natalie guiding her into exploring its dimensions.

A radiance has begun to creep into Lillian's face. She picks up another card, the Six of Cups that shows a woman in a long dress offering a bouquet of flowers to a kneeling man.

Lillian: "I want to be and do as I wish. I want to be able to be loving and cheerful without thinking there's anything wrong with it."

Then she puts down that card, and Natalie places it on top of Strength and The Star cards so that all are visible. Lillian looks through the cards one more time, moving them around with her fingers. She stops when she finds one that shows a woman standing on a sort of spire, holding a world globe in her hands, with a bird perched on it, called The World. "Here!" she says triumphantly. With this card I feel like the old ropes are fraying. I myself can choose how to be me."

A whole new world of possibilities is open. Her depression seems to have vanished, at least for the moment.

Natalie takes the card from her and sets it on top of the other cards so that all four are visible. Now there are two stacks a few inches from each other, one for Lillian's past and one for her present and future. "For now," Lillian says, "I feel good. I want to take a picture of these cards because they make me feel better about myself. They've just told me about my past and present and my possibilities." As she takes out her cell phone and snaps a photo of the cards, and then a selfie of herself holding the Strength card, she smiles.

Natalie, who conducted the session above, is a skilled Tarot reader who loves the cards. She is also a gestalt therapist with decades of experience. Using the cards in conjunction with her other therapeutic interventions allowed her to identify the roots of Lillian's problems more rapidly than she would otherwise have done. Toward the end of the session, she was able to use the cards to help Lillian construct a new emotional stack that provides a framework for the healing directions she sees her life taking.

Even if you feel that you would need to have psychological training to do what Natalie did, after some practice with the above methods, a good reader will have a sense of when one or another can be used appropriately and effectively. If you start to use one of those methods and it works, great. If not, you're likely to feel the person psychologically "backing away," and you can return to the comfort zone of conversing productively about what certain cards mean for that person.

Topdog and Underdog

In dialogues like the one with Lillian, typically the voice that represents one of the card's images will be strong and the other weak. Fritz Perls called these different parts of one's internal struggle the *topdog* and the *underdog*. Usually the card that represents your client is the underdog and the card representing the other person is the topdog. But not always. The client's own persona may be angry and assertive and the other person may be submissive, beaten down, and nearly voiceless.

Often, as the kind of projective dialogue described above proceeds, the underdog's voice gains power so that the two voices become more equal. When this happens, it's a key development, because typically the underdog is where a person's disowned strength lies. Topdog is frequently rigid and authoritarian. Underdog is commonly more flexible and creative, with an attitude of give and take.

From Stacks to Complexes

After you have some experience working with these methods, you might consider a somewhat different way to explore a stack.

When you're working with another person, sometimes you may intuit where the strongest emotional charge is even though the client hasn't said so. When this happens, at first the deeper feelings shown in the lower cards may be hidden. When the person discusses or identifies with and acts out each card, stronger or less obvious feelings may be revealed.

For some people in some situations, just finding and discussing cards that reflect the deeper dimensions of their inner worlds may be enough to bring a great and illuminating clarity to what had seemed confused and confusing.

For others such clarification highlights the elements of an inner or outer conflict, so that the person can begin working toward a healing transformation.

In ancient times the word "samskara" was used for such hidden qualities that shape our lives. This Sanskrit word refers to traces of past experiences that are part of our mind-body-emotion-action makeup. Everyone has many sanskaras or samskaras, (depending on which translation of the term you prefer). Here we arbitrarily choose sanskara.[1]

Psychiatrist Carl Jung noted that responses left over from past experience are not all created equal. Some stem from traumatic experiences. They may range from an infant almost starving due to not getting enough milk, to an adult surviving an airplane crash, or a battlefield firefight in which limbs were lost. Traumatic memories can live quietly dormant under the surface due to repression of suffering that was caused by pain, neglect, or beatings by parents or other authority figures or even peers—such as a sibling or the school bully—perhaps accompanied with words like, "You'd better stop crying or I'll really give you something to cry about." Jung coined the term "complexes" for such emotionally and mentally troublesome sanskaras, (later adopted by his colleagues Alfred Adler for the "inferiority complex" and Sigmund Freud for the "Oedipus complex" and "Electra complex.")[2]

A complex is an indication that there may be serious work to do. Often, this is best done by a therapist with specific expertise in handling post-traumatic stress disorders. But most of us also have numerous "mini-complexes" that do not seriously interfere with our lives, and that we can reduce by ourselves through such methods as self-guided relaxation and meditation. If you're a reader, you will see many of these mini-complexes—and be expected to help others find their ways out of them in your work with the cards.

Moving with sensitivity, understanding boundaries (your own and others), and not going where obvious signals say, "don't go" can be just as important to your reading of emotions as your skill in talking your client through their issue. Don't wade in too deeply, or try to swim through currents that are too strong for you to handle. (In some decks, a woman on the Temperance card has one foot on land and one foot in the water of a stream or pond. Tarot scholar Art Rosengarten reminds us of an ancient Chinese proverb, "When you want to test the depths of a stream, don't use both feet."[3]

If you're an experienced reader, you probably know what kind of work you can do, and how you can use your cards to assist the healing process. Even quick fixes in a short reading have value. On the other hand, working slowly but surely is often the best path, especially during a personal journey that involves resolving a challenging maze hidden within our unconscious self.

Experiencing Projective Dialogue
Now It's Your Turn

Pair up with another person. (It can be a friend who gives you permission to experiment with this technique.) For present purposes, we will imagine that you're working with a fellow professional. One of you will be the client, one the facilitator. After a set time, reverse roles. When to change is up to you and the other person.

First the person in the role of facilitator asks the client to choose two cards from the face-up deck. The first card will represent the client, and the second card stands for another person with whom he or she wishes to dialogue in order to work through a mental or emotional block or frustration. Through voice and body language, the client gives words to the images and lets the two cards "talk to each other." In doing this it is essential to alternate between the voices and gestures represented by the two different cards and roles. Encourage the client to be sensitive to his or her moment-by-moment awareness of thoughts, feelings, and sensations, such as tension, relaxation, or changes in breathing or anxiety as he or she talks back and forth between the two different cards.

The facilitator, looking on from the outside, may suggest when to "change" from the voice of one card to the other. If the person feels unready to change, or feels ready before the facilitator suggests it, he or she should follow his or her inclination. (If it feels appropriate, at some point the facilitator may tell the client, "Whenever you feel ready to change to being the voice of the person represented by the other card and want to reply from that position, go ahead, even if I haven't asked you to.")

One general rule is that whenever the client asks a question from the position of either card or the person it represents, the therapist or facilitator immediately suggests that the other card (or "person") reply. Besides the "answer the question" principle, as facilitator, let your sense of the situation's energy and emotional flow tell you when the client should switch from one voice that represents one card to being the other person represented by the second card.

Pay special attention to feelings. If the person is skipping over them and intellectualizing or talking just about behavior or the situation, ask again at what seem to be critical points, "How do you feel as you say (or do) that? Often when a person has felt something deeply, it is useful to have them put that experience into words. In contrast, when a person has described something well, it is useful to have them move into the feeling beneath the words, or express their feelings through body language.

Whether the person is enacting his or her own role or that of the other person within the role-playing "interaction," when he or she falls silent, allow a minute or two for reflection. Then you might say something such as, "Did anything else, any memory or feeling, come up during that quiet moment?" You can also ask, "Is there something you want to say but can't quite get out, whether or not it's related to the images in this card?"

Usually you will want to encourage a lively back-and-forth dialogue rather than long statements that border on monologues. Once the full dimensions of an issue have emerged, the statements are likely to grow shorter. Short statements often contain as much vital information as long ones. When the moment feels right, the facilitator may suggest, "Now say just one sentence each time you go back and forth between the voice represented by each card, until you're ready to stop." This quick and to-the-point dialogue often strips a situation down to its essence. After a few such lines, often what there was to say has been said and the person will spontaneously stop. If he or she can't move beyond wordy statements, it may mean that the person is stuck in one track of a "broken record" of thoughts and feelings replaying over and over again. But if the back and forth dialogue between two cards and the people or situations they represent continues with significant energy bursting forth, important new information and directions may emerge. If so, encourage the continuation of more dialogue.

By contrast, if the process does not lead to some kind of understanding or resolution in regard to the issue in question, and the client has unfinished or unresolved thoughts and feelings, the facilitator can have the person select another card that appears symbolically significant for their situation. Ask the client how the chosen card feels connected to his or her own dilemma. Is there anything left unfinished that will still need to be addressed?

Keeping a Record

You or your client or querent may wish to fill out this section (perhaps on a separate page) after you have experienced the type of session described above.

My Experience Using
A Projective Dialogue Method
(If you choose conversation rather than enactment and projective dialogue, fill in only the blanks for questions that are relevant to your experience.)

✏️ The card I chose to represent "the other person" is the:

_____
_____
_____
_____

✏️ The "what" and "how" of the way this card resembles "the other person" is:

_____
_____
_____
_____

✏️ When I discussed the interaction between the other person and myself, I became aware of feelings that include:

_____
_____
_____
_____

✏️ When I identified with the other, I felt and/or thought and/or sensed the following sensations in my body:

_____
_____
_____
_____

✏️ As if you were telling a story, when you pretend to be the voice for the other person, say out loud or write silently what you feel, sense and think about yourself from the perspective of that person:

_____
_____
_____
_____

✏ I act...

_____
_____
_____
_____

✏ I want . . .

_____
_____
_____
_____

✏ I have ...

_____
_____
_____
_____

✏ I want you to . . .

_____
_____
_____
_____

✏ When I enacted the other's way of holding his or her stance that may have included gesturing, speaking, standing, moving around, and noticing where I was looking, I learned . . .

_____
_____
_____
_____

✏ When I enacted my own way of being with that person (if I did so), I became more aware that . . .

_____
_____
_____
_____

✏️ The cards I selected for an emotional stack to represent the other person in this situation are:

_____

_____

_____

_____

✏️ The cards I selected for an emotional stack to represent myself in this situation are:

_____

_____

_____

_____

Two Cards, Two Messages

The more you practice giving representational readings, or using card imagery in your therapy, counseling, or coaching, the easier this process will become. If this procedure is totally new to you, we can compare learning to do representational readings with driving a car. When you first get behind the wheel, you drive cautiously, slowly, and may be somewhat confused as to what to do. After you've been driving longer, you drive with more confidence.

To have another sense of how to use the cards, let's briefly use them in a quite different way, one that is found in a divinatory reading. Fan your cards face down and without looking at the images, use your intuition to find a card that attracts your interest. Pull this one card to answer the question, "How can I best benefit from doing the Tarot exercises that I recently completed?"

What message did you find in the card you just pulled? What sense can you make of this card's message in relation to professionally using the techniques that you just experienced?

Now choose a card for yourself in relation to your personal life. Shuffle and cut your face-down cards and again fan them out on the table or in your hand with their backs toward you. Inwardly ask yourself the following question: "What can I do to pamper my inner spirit and enjoy life more?" Again, using your intuition, choose one card that you feel will provide an insightful answer to your question. After you look at it, take some time to ponder its symbolic answer. What does it suggest to you?

In both these cases, if you don't find a statement that makes sense try again and pull another until you find a useful message.

Whenever you work in almost any healing or other human services capacity, with or without the cards, self-care is of paramount importance. Worrying about others, trying to understand their concerns, and not taking time to take care of yourself depletes your mental energy. Make sure you find ways to balance work with pleasure, connect with your vitality, and take time to have fun. Hopefully this last card reading has offered some insight in how to take good care of yourself.

Now, get ready to dive a bit further into the depths of psyche as next we will be using the cards to explore contrasting sides of your own interior world. Is your deck ready?

7.

INNER DIALOGUES: CONVERSATIONS AMONG SIDES OF THE SELF

Do you ever want two different things but can't have them both? Or even want to avoid several unwanted alternatives when you have no choice but to accept one of them? Such dilemmas sometimes happen to everyone. The worries and concerns that go with them are part of the human condition. Ambivalence can be stressful, especially when lack of clarity breeds uncertainty and confusion about future directions. People often get so anxious about the fear of making the wrong decision that they can't choose at all. Discovering truths buried under uncertainties is a key to finding solutions to ambiguous choices.

Many people approach Tarot readers to see if the cards can bring clarity to their dilemma about which choice to make. Questions such as, "Should I marry Jim? Or should I break it off and move to New York?" are more common than not. To help a person hear their opposing voices more clearly and discern which choice is most attractive or holds the most promise, we offer the following Tarot practice.

From a face-up Tarot deck ask a person to choose two or more cards that represent sides of him or herself that want different things. In so doing, the person identifies one possible choice with one card and another potential choice with a different card. Each card represents a separate and conflicting voice that advocates one or another desired outcome. Having a person choose cards to represent the different sides of his or her internal dialogue is a powerful way to proceed when a person is in a conflict such as, "One side of me wants to go into investment banking and make big bucks like my father wants me to, while the other side says, 'I want to be a musician—screw materialism.'" This person might choose the King of Pentacles for the former side and theTwo of Cups for the latter.

Another person struggling with emotional issues might say, "I've fallen out of love with my husband and I want a divorce. I just don't see how we can get past some of the harshness of our past. But I'm afraid to leave as I have no idea how I would survive by myself."

You never know what challenges a person will bring to your table or consulting room, but it's good to have a method to work with questions that involve decision-making. Here's another example of ambivalent thinking when it can work well to have your client choose a card to represent each different voice: "I really don't know who I am. A lot of the time I feel confused. It's like three or four different people are living inside me and having an argument about how I should be and what I should do." With such a query, the person may select several cards, one for each diverse inner voice.

Sometimes it becomes obvious that the card chosen to represent one voice turns out to be an attitude or belief borrowed from someone else. In psycho-lingo, it's something "swallowed whole" but not "chewed and tasted thoroughly."[1] In that case, one card may end up representing an important person dwelling in your client's mind who has stated an expectation or desire that your client feels a need to fulfill. This might even be someone who has died, or is no longer in the person's life. In such a situation he or she could choose one card for his or her own inner voice, and also another card to be the other person who voices opinions or demands from "inside" his or her head.

Doing an "Inner Dialogue" Spread for Yourself

As usual, whenever possible we recommend that you try each technique for yourself before doing it with another person. If circumstances permit, please take a few minutes now to get out your cards and experiment with this spread.

Is there something you are of two minds about? Do you have any ambivalence that you've been struggling with? You might want to think of what choices you are facing while you lay out your cards. Once you have a situation in mind, pull two cards.

Card 1:
Scan through your face-up deck, and find a card with an image that evokes your sense of one side of your situation.

Card 2:
Find a different card with images that reflect the other side of your concerns.

Place the two cards side-by-side on the table or surface in front of you. Envision the images symbolizing your opposing feelings. Give each card a voice that expresses the inclination it represents, and what you think and feel about it. Let your initial statement that goes with each card, and your inner dialogue between them continue as long as necessary to hear each of the two or more sides of your personal story as clearly as possible.

If you don't think of any such issue right now, for the sake of learning from experience, pull the Major Arcana card The Chariot from your deck. Imagine yourself to be driving the chariot and looking at the path in front of you. In the image shown here, the white horse is pulling you toward the left, and the other toward the right.

In what directions are these two forces trying to move you? What, if anything, do they say to each other? Which choices do you need to make to keep your chariot moving on a beneficial path?

Seeing yourself as the driver of a chariot with horses pulling in different directions may help you create an "Inner Dialogue" spread for yourself or others. For example, you might pull two more cards to accompany The Chariot. One side of you might want to dive into worldly affairs, whether for personal gain or to further truth and justice, symbolized by your choice of the Six of Wands. A different part of you might identify with and select the major card the Hermit, as he appears to prefer a path of meditation and personal enlightenment, following his own wise inner spiritual guidance. Not necessarily an easy choice.

Using an "Inner Dialogue"
Reading for Others

You just read about, and hopefully created, an inner dialogue card spread for yourself. You can also use such a process when you have a client, querent, or even a friend who is caught in a force field of internal or external inclinations that are pushing or pulling in opposing directions.

When guiding another person in this process, once the person has described their dilemma, spread out the deck face up on the table. Ask the person to look through it, choose two or more cards with images that symbolize each different choice or conflicted aspect of him or herself, and place them in a straight row in front of your client. Then ask why each card was chosen, what impression the images convey, and what statement each one seems to make. Are any outside forces affecting the situation? Listen to hear if your client is being influenced by other people's attitudes, opinions, or demands.

Encourage the person to personally identify with each card or to become its voice and listen to its message. You may hear responses such as, "As the Magician (shown as "Hermes" in this deck), I can use my magic wand to get my partner to say yes to a trip to Europe."

Or when the Fool (shown as "Stultitia" in this deck) is chosen, "I want to be foolish for a while and say 'no' to my responsibilities. I'm tired of working all the time and worrying about paying bills."

A person who identifies with the Queen of Cups card in the next illustration might say, "She looks so peaceful. I want to hold a cup and offer nourishment to everyone around me." When the person has finished speaking, ask him or her to look at the cards again and find one that reflects a different part of him or herself. This different part may be in conflict with the side just described, or may be a side that is usually kept hidden, or that wants something different. It may even be uncertain in contrast to the other side's certainty. Ask the person to identify with this second card that is pulled to represent the conflicting stance. Here, for example, the person has chosen the Four of Pentacles linked with building a solid foundation to symbolize feelings that are very different from the Queen of Cups. Again leave a brief period for reflection, and if just two cards were chosen you might want to ask, "Do these two cards sum up the situation, or do you want to choose one, or even more than one, additional card to look further into what is going on?" When people want to choose one or two more cards, give them time to do so. Whatever other associations are offered, by asking "What do you sense and feel in your body at this very moment as you say these things?" you will

most likely increase your sense of what is happening in the person's psyche.

After the two cards are initially discussed, you can proceed by asking the person to carry out a back-and-forth dialogue between the different sides of the self as reflected by the various cards. You might ask:

- "Is one card more like your usual view of yourself and one card dramatically different?"
- "What are the two different roles that are being portrayed?"
- "Do you tend to give one side greater importance or more respect?"
- "Does one seem to have more power? If so, what does the other side feel and say about that?"
- "How do you feel if you turn completely away from what is represented in card two and ignore its potential? . . . or if you turn completely away from what is represented in card one?"

Follow your inclinations about how to guide the person's process, and also be forthright in checking your hunches. For instance, if you're sensing that something is left out of their card's dialogue, you might say something like, "It sounds to me like you haven't mentioned something important—is that possible?"

Continue with your discussion until the dialogue reaches some resolution, or until it's clear that no resolution is likely now. In the latter case, you can ask the person to summarize where the two sides stand in regard to each other. What are the present dimensions of the internal conflict? Or, what is the current emerging struggle? When you are nearing closure, you can offer a summary yourself if you seem to sense one, and then ask, "Is that accurate?" If not, you might say, "What am I missing or getting wrong?"

During this process, if you are familiar with the card meanings, or if you see something in a card that appears connected to the client's concern, you can mention it and ask whether your idea is relevant. If the answer is "Yes" or "Maybe," then you can ask questions to inspire further reflection. In such inner dialogues, remember the principle of emotional stacks. An inclination may have several different feelings associated with it. Additional cards can be chosen to introduce more possibilities and fathom what lies beneath the surface.

The Wisdom Card

When working with a client, you may sometimes find a brief "wisdom card statement" a useful way to conclude. After the inner dialogue spread described just prior, you can choose one more card to complete your session. This final card to be selected by your client represents a medicine woman, shaman, wise old man, guardian angel, *kahuna*, guru, or minister, or any other figure you "both" imagine may potentially add words of wisdom to your present dilemma. For now, let's imagine that the High Priestess ("Sybil" in this deck) has been chosen to serve this function. Center the High Priestess above the cards representing the voices whose views are in conflict. As facilitator for this reading you can inwardly or outwardly ask for additional clarity or insight from the guardian represented by this card, but your client will be the voice for her wisdom. Ask your client to identify with the figure and speak out loud the statement this guardian wants to share that hasn't already been included in the discussion of the inner dialogue spread. Your client might say, "As Mother of Light and Compassion, what I want you to know right now about this situation is . . ." and then continue speaking, unrehearsed, letting whatever comes cascade uninterruptedly from his or her mouth like the flow of the River of Life itself. Listen carefully to hear whether this expands the client or querent's understanding of the topic of their reading or counseling session.

If you are doing a reading for yourself, you will be the voice for this wisdom figure, and speak individually to each of your inner card-selves who have been involved in dialogue. Once the final words have been spoken, reflect on what you just heard your voice say and how your mind, body, and emotions are responding.

Sometimes this card will shed light on how to make sense of polarities, and turn opposition and struggles into hopeful directions. If someone selects a card that negates any possible interpretation of how to read a potentially useful direction into a situation, you can take control of the closing direction of the session, say, "Not that one," and choose the final card yourself. For the best outcome, select one that you can discuss in relation to meaningful options and positive possibilities. If you've been listening carefully to the spontaneous messages given by the person when he or she discussed each card, you will probably be able to offer something of value. If, from your own perspective, there's something you want to add to the client's closing statement, feel free to do so because, as facilitator, you're expected to do that.

Hearing Your Own Subliminal Messages through Freestyle Writing

One way to let the cards help you hear—and perhaps transform—your statements to yourself is through writing. This creative undertaking can be done simply by noticing brief snippets of your thoughts and feelings that are triggered by the images on a card. Then, what usually works best is for you to write your reactions in a *freestyle* mode (called "free writing" by some writing teachers).[2]

To do this practice, first, from your face-up deck, choose two cards with images that represent different sides of your internal dilemma or conflict. Using a pen and paper (or keyboard), give each differing voice a name or even just a letter, such as A and B. Next, write the first name or initial of one of the cards you chose on your paper and jot down your thoughts in relation to it as fast as you can. Let whatever ideas flow through your mind come out quickly in writing, even if they seem like a total sitcom and irrelevant to your dilemma.

Then on a new line, write the name of the other card or the voice it represents, and rapidly write whatever thoughts, feelings, sensations, and inclinations to action it evokes. Don't be long-winded. It's best to move back and forth with your statements from one image to the other and vice-versa in short crisp sentences or phrases. Move down to a new line each time you change voices (or cards) as if you are an author writing a dialogue. In the example below, Adam chose the Seven of Wands for "Risky Adam" and the Temperance card for "Careful Adam."

Risky Adam (RA) *is portrayed by the Seven of Wands:*
"I want that new convertible so bad I can almost taste it."

Careful Adam (CA) *is symbolized by Temperance:*
"I can't afford it, I'm already in over my head with student loans, and it's just crass materialism."

RA: *(Seven of Wands)*: "But all the babes would love to ride around in it, and just think how much my love life would improve."

CA: *(Temperance)*: "It wouldn't make any difference to someone who really cares about me, and besides, this is all just mind garbage. I don't know if there's even any point in doing this writing because this garbage stinks."

RA: *(Seven of Wands):* "You're right. There's probably no point in it at all, except that getting a hot girl to go with a hot car would be great."

CA: *(Temperance):* "What point is there in anything? I want a girl that wants me, not my car."

If you were Adam writing your dialogue, after a few minutes, put down your pen and read what you just wrote. You can mentally summarize what you said and weigh the pros and cons of your situation as you wrote them. You have given specific form to elements flowing from what psychologist William James referred to as your "stream of consciousness."

When doing your writing exercise, after you choose cards that reflect your different feelings or inclinations write your inner dialogue for at least ten minutes. Write as quickly and spontaneously as you can. Then after you have taken five more minutes to reflect on what you've written; you might even choose to repeat this process once or twice to gain greater clarity. But don't do it more than twice, as your energy for it will probably begin to wane.

Writing as fast as you can without pausing to think can open a channel to your subconscious mind. Thoughts and feelings you didn't know you had will sometimes bubble up "between the cracks" of your conscious thoughts. When you do this exercise, sometimes you're likely to find that you gain insights that resolve your dilemma. Other times you may come to a deeper understanding of yourself or feelings you have about other people or matters involved in your situation. We can't tell you specifically what you will learn from your written dialogue with the cards, but usually you will gain something of value.

A "Window on Your Inner World" Five-Card Spread

At times you or your client may get bogged down in analyzing internal arguments about one thing or another, or in weighing the validity of different choices. Or your situation might demand a truly innovative approach. When you seek to respond creatively to a dilemma that has no obvious solution, you might combine divinatory and representational uses of the cards. This gives you, the reader or counselor, more say in

115

how to interpret and communicate the cards' import. With this procedure you need some familiarity with meanings of the symbols on each card.

You can use any spread you think will work best. Here we offer the example of using a five-card spread in which the cards are laid in a horizontal row to explore the parameters of either an inner dilemma or an outer situation.

To begin your reading for another, ask your client to think of an important issue or question, which he or she may or may not choose to reveal to you. Without looking at card images, either you or your client will shuffle the deck. Ask your client to cut the cards to create five face-down stacks in a horizontal row. As you turn over the top card of each stack, you will be viewing an imagery-rich map that will be used as a medium to inspire reflection and discussion. Depending on the question(s), you may be looking for insight about where he or she might be headed now or hope to go in life. The following is a list of descriptive phrases for each card position in this spread.

The Five-Card "Inner World" Spread

CARD	Card Spread Position Meanings
CARD 1	What do I feel now?
CARD 2	What do I want or need?
CARD 3	What (internal or external) central influences or challenges am I facing?
CARD 4	My present choices
CARD 5	What work do I need to do to help myself find the best solution or answer to my question?

For example, you might draw these five cards:

We have intentionally not suggested interpretations for the five images shown in this spread so that you can react with your own personal responses. For you, right now, what do these five images in the "Inner World" spread suggest to you personally? In other words, how would you interpret the image on the card The Lady of Swords in relation to the first card position that represents "What do I feel now?" Next, how would you discuss the Three of Wands in relation to the second position that represents the question, "What do I want or need?" What feelings emerge when you compare these first two cards? Now, how might you discuss the Five of Swords in relation to its spread position concerning the question, "What central influences or challenges am I facing?" Are you getting a sense about the direction these cards are pointing? What are your ideas about The Three of Cups in relation to the fourth card position titled, "My present choices?" How does this card relate to the previous three cards? And what do you imagine is the best way to discuss The Three of Pentacles in relation to the final card position representing the inquiry, "What work do I need to do to help myself find the best solution or answer to my question?" Right now, can you think of answers for these questions?

What path of personal action or discovery, if any, does this spread suggest to you? How would you interpret the cards for an emotional versus a career question? Since this is an example of a divinatory spread with cards drawn from a face-down deck, some of your insights may be surprising, and perhaps informative in unexpected ways. (If a card within the spread makes no sense in relation to its question, then if you have a deck nearby you can set that card aside and pull another that may be more informative or meaningful.)

When in a working session with another person, keep track of your or your client's personal revelations as you dialogue. What tendencies and inclinations surface in what is being revealed to you by the card images and by your client's feedback? Even silence has something to say.

Examine each card's image as a single clue that might reveal something about the synergy of the combined group of five cards. Then think about whether this particular group of five cards, when viewed together, convey some message. For example, three of the five are "threes." Does that suggest anything to you? Because this type of reading combines divinatory and representational reading techniques, you can discuss any relevant insights that connect with a person's present reactions to a card's image, or with its traditional meaning, or both. Can you find any new angle or avenue suggested by these cards?

When you've finished discussing (or even identifying with and/or enacting) potential messages from the cards in this spread, you can ask the person what feels most relevant if it is not obvious by then. Even if you are the ultimate authority of a card's meaning when you're the person in charge of doing the work, you can work together with the client or querent to find useful solutions to challenging situations. The healing of the heart is more important than having "correct" interpretations of symbols.

Also, when using the cards to describe possibilities, sometimes you can pull one card to represent or "divine" what may be coming next in someone's life. For example, just now I pulled the Wheel of Fortune.

A wheel is a symbol for movement and traveling along the road of life. I'm interpreting this card as telling me that it's time to move on. We've seen how to use discussion, identification, and projective dialogues with another person, and how to use them to explore the "inner dialogues" between or among different parts of the self. Now we move to ways of working with larger groups of people who are in some kind of relationship with each other. At one extreme this may be two others, such as two parents, roommates, siblings, or friends. At the other extreme it may be groups that are relatively large and complex and include many people, like an office staff or a large family, as you are about to see.

2 OF CUPS

8.

—

MULTIPLE OTHERS, THE CARDS, AND YOU

Ah, a bouquet of flowers, a glass of wine, a loving touch, and thou! How sweet are such moments! Think of a mother's unconditional love and concern for her children, and other family members' love for one another. But there is also the other side: hostility, antagonism, and bitter feuds between one person and another. Sorting through complicated mazes of emotions is one of the central tasks that occur in both psychological work and in readings.

In our daily lives and our emotional connections, often we interact with not just one person, but with two or even several others at once. Surely at times you've been with two or more people when you wanted to share your feelings but held back.

We're hoping that at this point you have a good sense of how to use the cards to help someone illuminate important dimensions of a relationship with another person, and that you can use them to clarify differing inclinations within yourself. Now we're going to provide sample sessions that show how to use them to shed light on what's going on in interactions and relationships that involve several people—whether as few as three or as many as a dozen or more. This is a more advanced continuation and expansion of earlier techniques. First we look at the communication and behavior of three people who are involved with each other. Then we move to a larger group focus. Finally we look at using card imagery that involves several others in sessions with children and teenagers.

An Emotionally Charged Session with a Client and Her Parents

Starting with just three people, a classical example of work with multiple others is a child's relationship with parents who act in emotionally damaging ways toward the child. Often one parent is abusive and the other one knows exactly what is happening but feels helpless or afraid and does nothing to stop it.

For example, Johanna's father had an anger and violence problem. At times he beat her or her sister severely, sometimes hitting her with a belt or other object, and on a few occasionally he would even kick one or the other of them, bruising their bodies and crushing their spirits. His blows were loud and unmistakable, yet when such incidents occurred, their mother was nowhere to be seen. She knew the warning signs that such an incident was coming, and when it did, always managed to be somewhere else. In the privacy of a consulting room, Johanna was asked to choose cards with images that represent her feelings concerning significant others involved in her emotional dilemma. They are placed randomly on the table. Here's a Tarot card portrait of her family that she chose from a face-up deck: The two top cards are her father and mother and the bottom card is Johanna.

Choosing Cards to Represent More Than One Significant Other

Using the *Tarot of the Boroughs*, Johanna chose The Four of Swords to illustrate how she feels in her family. Her father in his white suit (The Hierophant) shows a fine front to the world and conceals his abuse of his family. The Nine of Swords reflects her mother's powerlessness and fear in regard to her husband.

In the working session, at first Johanna was tentative and quiet when she was asked to identify with and speak as the voice of the card she chose for herself. With encouragement to express her feelings, quietly and tentatively at first, the card she chose for herself told "Dad" what a bully and coward he was. Then she screamed the cruel details of her perceptions. She went on to describe in detail how his behavior had emotionally scarred both her and her brother. Then she turned to address her mother.

THE HIEROPHANT

9 OF SWORDS

4 OF SWORDS

"And you, Mom! Busying yourself by always managing to be in another room or gone somewhere when we kids needed your help. Why didn't you protect us? You knew what Dad was doing! I never heard you say a word to stop him. Couldn't you even have said, 'Mike, please don't do that. You're hurting her.' You should have done something!"

Johanna was half-talking, half-sobbing, but as she continued, her voice grew stronger. Then the facilitator asked her to change viewpoints and become the voice of the card she had chosen as her mother. Her imagined mom started talking about her own terror and her own childhood abuse. Repeatedly the victim, she had never learned how to

Past   **Present**   **Future**

confront others or handle a charged situation. Then after role-playing her mother, Johanna became willing to play the part of her father, which initially was all about denial and distraction. Only after a tear-filled silence did she finally open up to a dialogue in which "he" admitted to feeling angry at the world, of feeling humiliated by others, of drinking too much, and of realizing how brutally wrong his actions had been. Sadly, even now in his daily life the hard, unrepentant facade is all he shows. When Johanna finally realized that her father's pattern was unlikely to change, her tears began to flow unmercifully.

Johanna's remarks are centered on her individual relationship with each of her parents, and with both of them together. She herself is the central focus.

Although Johanna's work demonstrates using two cards to represent two significant others, this same process can be used with multiple cards for several people who are involved with each other. Ultimately it's all about your client (in this example it's Johanna), but the focus of discussion may change in relation to the needs of the moment. Be prepared to stay focused on the chosen cards and not digress too far from the central issue unless a new one bursts through with greater energy.

As we will see in a moment, in a related but different kind of session, the client might be a background figure and the relationship between others who are involved is the central dynamic. Then the cards that represent the others and their interaction with one another become where the action is.

Before we continue, however, for the sake of a broader perspective, let's step back for just a moment and look at traditional divinatory readings. Many card readers sometimes use three-card spreads that include discussion of "the past" or foundation, "the present" or the now, and "the future" or resolution card.

Without being given an interpretation for these three cards, can you imagine the story they tell?

In general, the past card can represent the previously formed foundation of your client or querent's situation, the present card can be a reference point for what's happening now in relation to his or her concerns, and the third card points toward a potential direction or outcome of present actions.

Even though this three-card layout frequently represents the past, present, and future, when doing sessions with three-card spreads your discussion doesn't have to involve predictions. Rather, this card layout can look at the past foundation that has already been created in relation to what the person needs to do now, in the present, to create the future he or she wants. Or it can bring to the surface insights that are hidden from obvious view. Its purpose can be to expand the client's inner awareness and their understanding of what goes on in their interactions with others who are important in their life. In some situations, you'll probably conclude that labels different from past, present, and future do a better job of capturing the essence of a situation. You can use whatever designations you think will be most useful.

The "Spectator Spread"

Three cards also have the potential to expand the client's understanding of what goes on between others even when they themselves are not interacting with them. For the latter situation we suggest using the Spectator Spread. This method is especially useful when you have witnessed the interactions between a client and others and the main dynamic in the situation is still a mystery. When doing the Spectator Spread ask your client to select three cards from a face-up deck. (In this example we're assuming that there are just two other people involved in this situation.) Simply lay the selected cards in a horizontal row. From right to left the card positions are:

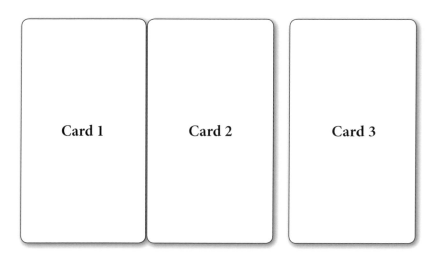

Card 1:
The Primary or Most Significant Other

Card 2:
The Secondary Principal Other

Card 3:
The Self

In this illustration the card that represents the self is separated from the other two by an empty space. This placement symbolizes the person's own self playing the function of a silent observer, saying nothing to the other two (or more) cards as they "interact" with each other. Depending on the situation being discussed by your client or querent, his or her role can be active or passive in relation to igniting the interaction between the two people represented by the other cards.

In the following example we'll assume that a young man selects card one for Mom, Dad is card two, and card three is himself, and they are placed on the table.

First he is guided to identify with card one that represents Mom, and enacts her way of holding herself, moving, speaking, and acting in the world. Then he is asked to play her role as she interacts with Dad, card two, and act as much like her as he can. Next he is asked to switch roles and to identify with the card that reflects Dad and enact Dad's way of

being as he responds to Mom. But, represented by card three, the client does not speak to or interact with either parent. He is a "spectator" to their interaction—hence the name of the spread.[1] Their dramatized interaction continues back and forth in this way for as long as the person wants to continue the role-playing dialogue—but probably not more than a few minutes. Meanwhile the facilitator gets a good look at each person's—in this case each parent's— ways of acting toward the other.

The following example is taken from a real-life session using this method with a young man, Jack, whose stated problem was a lack of initiative and energy. Jack chose The Star card to be Mom, the Magician to be Dad, and the Seeker, equivalent of The Fool to represent himself.

Jack began with a projective dialogue (as described in Chapter 6) between his own card and the one representing Mom. It offered no clue as to why he felt so much ongoing lethargy. Nor did the dialogue between him and his father's card. The therapist was puzzled.

Then he was asked to carry out a dialogue, complete with any accompanying body language, between the card representing Mom and the card corresponding to Dad, while his own voice indicated by card three remained silent and separate. "He" watched and listened from a safe distance at the same time he was enacting a projective dialogue between Mom and Dad. When the cards that represented the two parents "interacted with each other," Mom turned out to be a commanding, authoritarian, spotlight-hogging figure. Dad meekly did whatever she ordered and got put down if he tried to carry out any ideas or initiatives

125

of his own. Suddenly, the source of the young man's behavior was crystal clear. In his life he was imitating the way Dad behaved with Mom.

This kind of session is not restricted to relations with parents. The "spectator" mode can be used with any pair (or even three or four) "others" whose interaction is a concern.

The "Insight-Gathering Spread" for Unveiling Complex Interpersonal Dynamics

Inevitably, we almost all find ourselves in groups of friends, co-workers, or family members in which multiple interactions occur at the same time. Instead of choosing cards that represent parents, as in the earlier examples, a person might select cards that represent siblings, friends, roommates, or any other collection of two or more other people who reflect a problem or opportunity. For instance, cards might be chosen for two or perhaps several co-workers who talk about team spirit but act competitively, or roommates who are encouraging a fellow student with poor grades to get drunk with them every night instead of studying.

When someone chooses images that stand for interactions with multiple others, they might pick one card for each person or one that represents two or even several people. With your guidance, cards can be chosen with images that inspire telling the story of how a person handles complicated interpersonal dynamics, and even conflicts.

First ask the person to select an image to represent him- or herself, and then a card for each other person who is involved. Each card that is chosen to represent people who strongly or frequently interact with your client is placed near the card representing the client. The cards that indicate people who have less influence in the client's situation are placed farther from his or her card. The following illustration using the Insight-Gathering Spread shows the dynamics of an office staff as viewed by my client, Sylvia, who has positioned cards from a face-up deck in relation to her feelings about her relationship with each other person.

First Sylvia, the project manager, chose The Page of Cups to represent herself, and put it in the center of the table. I asked her to select cards for the other workers with whom she talked regularly. To represent both her boss and his executive secretary she chose one card, the Two of Coins, which shows two people. For the accountant, she pulled the Three of Wands.

Then she chose cards to represent co-workers with various roles (sales, design, the receptionist, etc.) who get along well, like each other, and interact frequently, and placed them to the right of her own card. For the receptionist who acts as "communication central," the Nine of Cups was an easy choice. For sales and advertising, she selected the Queen of Cups, and for design, the Seven of Wands.

Finally, her relationships were more or less neutral with the computer whiz, the production manager, the purchasing and procurement manager, and the orders and shipping department—all shown in the bottom row.

With a few comments from Sylvia about why she selected specific cards, a quick glance at her spread revealed that opening better communication channels could reduce some of her problems at work. In turn, her increased clarity about how she was with her co-workers led not only to more productive interaction with them but also helped her become more insightful about her feelings and actions in other settings.

This free-form card layout and its exploration can be used in many different social contexts.

For many of us, the family is more central to our lives than any other social situation. Because we all have different experiences in our homes, let's take a moment to look through the magnifying glass of experience at how this kind of imagery work can be helpful with a family. In the following demonstration session, you are about to meet Heather, who has a tough time dealing with her family's challenging relationships. Because families are so important to most people, we have borrowed the name from family constellation work.

The "Family Constellation Spread" to Illuminate Family Dynamics

When using the cards to depict a family's structure and process, we introduce a few additional features. In the following session we see Heather's picture of her extended family. Heather was asked to position the cards to reflect the closeness or distance she feels with each person, and their closeness to or distance from each other. Cards can be placed at an angle or even upside down to reflect the unique character of a person's relationships with another person, or all the others. For instance,

if a card is placed upside down, it indicates that some aspect of the relationship it represents needs to be set straight. If someone is dead, the corresponding card is turned face down.

Heather chose The Moon to represent herself and placed it at the bottom of her spread to show her disconnection from most of her family. Scanning the cards Heather chose, we see Dad represented by the Two of Swords because he turns a blind eye and a deaf ear to whatever is going on in his family that he doesn't want to acknowledge. Heather settled on the Six of Coins ("Pentacles" in many decks) for Mom, who is at her wit's end about how to handle her out-of-control family. Heather portrays her older sister who is always complaining that she doesn't have what she wants as the Five of Wands and turns the card on its side because her sister's manipulative behavior makes it hard for Heather to connect with her. Grandma (The Queen of Cups) and Grandpa (The Emperor) are placed in the next row up, along with a younger sister, the Six of Wands. Their cards are separated to show the present coolness in their relationship. An aunt shown as the Page of Wands is a pole dancer and is viewed as the family's "black sheep." And Heather places in the top row the Ten of Swords, for her brother, the lost soul junkie, and the Knight of Swords for a sister who barely maintains a connection with the family.

In her working session, Heather began by saying that she hoped to improve her relationship with her parents. Then she went on to a series of "mini-dialogues" in which she briefly enacted the essence of her relationship with each of the family members depicted by the cards. Finally, she discussed the roles she felt that each person played, using pairs of cards to show the essence of what the family members said and felt toward one another. In other words, she let each pair of cards have a very brief conversation with each other while she herself was a "spectator" to it.

She said she seldom talked with the sister shown at the far left—Lacie, the Six of Wands. They shared a brief phone call once every couple of months—nothing more. But as Heather continued her discussion of the "family members' pictures," she found no opening with her mother or father. They were both chained to their existing attitudes. Of all the family members, Heather found herself talking more and more about how much she appreciated Lacie. At the end of the session, she was calling her on her cell phone as she realized that she had a more trusting relationship with her than with anyone else in the family. Heather had concluded that her interaction with her parents, and with most of the family, was, at least for now, not likely to change much. But she had clarified her own thoughts and awareness of the family dynamics. Quite unexpectedly, the beginning of a more open relationship with Lacie turned out to be the most valuable thing that came out of the session.

Testing These Methods for Self-Discovery

The following card layout gives you an opportunity to experience some of the methods used in the sessions described above. Take five minutes now to choose three (or even more) cards from a face-up deck and set them in front of you. Let two or more represent "others" from a group that you are part of. They can represent kindred spirits, emotional entanglements, antagonists, or . . . Without much forethought, make a statement from your heart that tells why you chose each card for the person it represents. What mental pictures, thoughts, and feelings are evoked by the card's imagery? Then let your creative imagination come alive and allow the image or images on each card reply to your statements. You might benefit from an internal dialogue about incidents that feel unfinished, and potentials for the future. What, if any, patterns or insights emerge from these dialogues?

Working with Children or Teens

Children and teenagers can benefit just as much as adults from exploring the card images and experiencing projective dialogues. In the world there are innumerable situations and countless types of dialogues.

One kind involves a group unified as a single entity, such as the school bully and his or her group of peers who intimidate or try to humiliate others. In a representational reading that involves such a situation, after a child or teen has told what he or she feels and thinks about it, a projective dialogue through pertinent cards that he or she has selected to represent the others may be useful.

First have the person project on to the troublesome other or others his or her own best guess about what's going on inside them, and then speak and act as if the guess is right. Encourage a back-and-forth dialogue. This may include what has actually gone on in the past, what is felt in the present, and concerns about the future. Probably not all guesses about what's going on with those in the adversary group that is belittling or intimidating will be correct, but that's okay. It opens up an opportunity to let out feelings that may have been tightly kept inside.

Let's look at an example of a representational reading with a teenager using the technique of a projective dialogue. First the adolescent agrees to explore his or her feelings about the "known others." Ask this person to choose cards for the several others who have something in common, such as a group of friends or opponents, and lump them all together on the table. Then have him or her look through your deck images and pick one card to represent him- or herself and place it at a distance from the other cards. Next, let the teen have her or his card talk to all those whose cards have been lumped together as if they were one person, speaking to whatever they have in common.

For example Earl, an early adolescent high school boy, chooses the Justice card to represent himself because he feels treated unjustly most of the time. He frequently faces a small group of "others" who get together and carry out various kinds of bullying tactics against him. He chooses The Fool to represent the others. Typically he withdraws and silently "takes" their physical or verbal abuse, not seeing what he can do about it. With the cards that he has laid out, he begins to role-play "them" as a group and says derisively,

"Hey look—here comes wimpo. Did 'jer grandma get those clothes you've got on at the nuthouse or did you steal them off a corpse?" (They all laugh or snicker.)

Looking dejected, Earl says that often something will happen like one person in the group will come forward, shove him off balance, then quickly move back to be with the other bullies.

You can ask him to notice, or at least think about, how he may be contributing to making himself powerless. This probably includes words, body language, and action. Your constructive discussion may help him discover and let go of his part in acting vulnerable.

"Okay," you might say. "Now let your card speak and tell them what you'd really like to say. And remember that they're not actually here—you can say anything you want and they can't hurt you. Give it a try!"

Earl re-imagined himself as the Justice card wanting justice. He pretended that he was taking off his blindfold. "All right. You fucking hotshots! You may think you're cool when you push me around, but I see you as ugly and disgusting and a lot of other kids do, too. And you're a bunch of chickens, when it takes five of you to pick on one of me. And then, touching the Justice card, Earl says, "If you ever hurt me again, I'll get you alone one at a time, and use my sword to show you what kind of a wimp I am."

He let out his breath and dropped his shoulders. "Whew. Maybe I shouldn't have said that."

"As I said earlier," the facilitator replied, "in this room it's okay to say whatever you want to say. Everyone sometimes has feelings that they're smart enough not to act on. The Justice card represents strength of mind and staying inwardly balanced. I hope you can see yourself in the Justice card in a positive way and get more in touch with your strength. I believe you're too kind-hearted to use a sword against someone. Words don't have to become actions."

"Thanks for saying that. You make me feel better about myself. And that Justice card really did jump out and ask me to pick it."

When looking at Earl's process, you can see that letting the card images speak is sometimes easier than trying to have an emotionally closed young person make a personal statement without them. During such a session, you can also ask the person to choose one or more cards to be "allies" who would make related statements that would support him (or her). Then the client would take a turn at being each ally, and voice each card's encouragement. For instance, Earl might choose the Queen of Swords as an ally, and speaking through her, tell the cards that represent the bullies, "One more thing, if you feel good only when you make others feel small, you must feel pretty small yourself. You ought to get some help. You need it."

And then yet another card ally might make an altogether different kind of statement. This process can be compared to assertiveness training in which a person tries out role-playing specific actions modeled by others that may connect with his or her personal power.

Using Images to Represent Multiple Others—A Summary

The list below notes the techniques described just above. Unless you are doing a specific spread, ask the person to choose from a face-up deck as many cards as he or she feels are needed to represent members of his or her family or others involved in the pending group issue or circumstance.

1. In general, have your client or querent pull only cards for people who are significant in their life, like their best friend, lover, important business associate, etc.
2. When having your person pull cards for family members, include everyone.
3. The person chooses a card to represent him- or herself.
4. Have your person arrange the cards so that the cards for the people who are supportive of him or her are close to the client's own card. Position the cards of those from whom they feel anger, grief, or other painful feelings farther from your client's own card. After this process the cards will show a visual and representational configuration of how specified people affect your client's life. Lay down the cards; they can be placed at whatever angle seems to best reflect the client's relationship with them.

5. Once selected, cards are face up on the table. You can ask the person for one or two brief sentences (no more than three) that describe their associations with the images, their feelings about each card, and their relationship to the person who is represented by each card. Ask that their description include something about mental, emotional, or physically stressful associations.

We suggest that you take a few minutes to try this process for yourself before you go on to the next chapter, as your personal experience is a wonderful guide. Once you turn the page you'll be looking at, and encouraged to think about, some important points to keep in mind while doing this kind of imagery work.

Queen of Swords

9.

—

POINTS IN THE PROCESS

Do you sometimes wonder how to improve your working sessions? Most of us seek ways to enhance our abilities and improve our work. We're going to make a few suggestions that can make Tarot work a bit easier. Some are most appropriate in divinatory readings, some in counseling or therapy, and some in both. Some are valuable when you need to make quick appraisals of a person, such as in a ten-minute party or New Age reading, while others require a longer session.

Consider Beginning with a Mini-Meditation

Before you begin your session, it can be useful to practice some kind of mini-meditation, or at least take a few moments to center yourself. If you don't already have a centering or grounding meditation, you can use this following exercise if it appeals to you.

Take a few moments to close your eyes. Breathe a long, deep breath and affirm: "My mind is relaxing with every breath. I am surrounded by protective, cosmic light (prana) and grounded in this moment." Envision a stream of radiant healing light coming from heaven into the crown of your head. Inwardly watch it go downward through your body and out the soles of your feet like a deep root connecting your energy with the earth.

You can mentally repeat the above affirmation as many times as needed until you feel relaxed and centered within yourself. You can change it whatever way you please. Other affirmations you might try are:

- "I breathe in relaxation and awareness, I breathe out stress;"
- "I breathe in focused attention, I breathe out distraction" or;
- "With every breath I connect more fully with my soul guidance."

High Priestess

Synchronizing your affirmation with the rhythm of your breathing will help reduce distractions and balance your mind.

Alternatively, in gestalt therapy it is common practice to begin a session with both therapist and the client or clients (in a group session) speaking one sentence that begins with the words, "Now I am aware of . . . " as a way to center oneself and bring attention from the there and then to the here and now. The therapist emphasizes that the phrase is, "Now I am aware of . . . " and not "Now I am aware that . . ." Use of the single word "that" rather than "of" often leads the person into a conceptual statement about past, future, or some other there-and-then. It defeats the intent of bringing attention into this moment, right here, right now.

Identifying with or Distancing Yourself from Your Client

Sometimes you may find it hard to get a sense of where the person "is at." His or her psychological interior may not be easily visible or accessible. Two simple steps can often help you get a better sense of someone. First, imagine that the chair you are sitting in is very large. (You can do this even if it's actually quite small.) In your chair you can slide sideways or forward toward the client so that you are closer to his or her "space." Having your physical spaces closer together can also bring your psychological spaces closer together. With a heightened feeling of closeness, which often tends to encourage self-disclosure, you can also increase your sensitivity to the person's vibrations and energy field.

But as you move into the session, you may find that you become so emotionally identified with the person and his or her issue that you have a hard time separating yourself enough to work effectively. Metaphorically, you can't pull someone out of a deep hole if you're also down there in it. At that point you want to do the opposite of creating "closeness." You want a clear sense of yourself as separate and distinct from the other person. Unobtrusively slide sideways or backward in your chair or on your cushion until you are as far from your client as you can reasonably get. Find a posture and way of sitting that is clearly your own. You might even lean your upper body backward a bit. Strive to get a sense of the person in the context of his or her life-space, and sense your separateness from him or her.

Secondly, you can unobtrusively move into a posture and position that mirrors as closely as possible the way the person is sitting or holding him- or herself. Mirroring that physical position may well give you insight about his or her psychological position, too.

These subtle physical forms of approaching and distancing yourself from someone can be helpful. However, if you are empathic and working intuitively, you may want to merge as much as possible with the other person's energy field to understand most fully what is important and how he or she is holding their Qi, or life energy, both internally and externally. Such a reading is best done if you have been trained to use your intuitive abilities in this manner. Therapists are seldom trained as psychic readers and psychic Tarot readers are seldom trained as therapists. Rely on your own background and knowledge in order to connect with the person in the way that works best for you.

The Not-So-Obvious Inner World

Moon

An outlook that can not only be useful but sometimes even indispensable is that of trying to grasp and feel what the person's inner world is like prior to your attempts to conceptualize it. In doing so you are trying to understand this person's experience as he or she lives it, and then frame your discussion in terms of his or her own outlook. Psychologists call this approach "phenomenology." Readers call this approach doing a psychic reading. Since we relate to others through our own perceptions, it's all too easy to draw a curtain of misunderstanding between you and another person's different mode of relating to life.

Although language is often abstract, if we can find very specific words and phrases to mirror what we hear the other person saying, we can come closer to grasping how their experience is for them.

French philosopher Maurice Merleau-Ponty spoke of trying to find a "first opening" on another's world that is free of our personal interpretations or perceptions.[1] Such perceptions are often but not always judgmental. Everything you perceive as reality seen, heard, or sensed through the mediating filters of your mind and body may or may not be accurate. It may be somewhat accurate and somewhat off the mark.

Seeking to reduce the interference of our preconceptions, Merleau-Ponty sought to hear what another person's subjective world was truly like for that person. What most of us usually do instead is to pass another person's statements through our own mental and emotional filters. When we work with images, one set of such filters is our learned associations about the meanings of each card. But for most of us, hearing another's reality without filtering it through our own unconscious distortions is a challenging task.

Fortunately, the phenomenologists developed a method to lessen this problem. They call it *bracketing*. Here's how to do it with the cards.

First, ask the person to select a card or cards from either a face-up or face-down deck, as fits the situation. Then ask how the images relate to their life. Your task is to listen to their comments and *notice every time a thought, memory, fear, approval or disapproval, or other feeling is evoked in you by what they say.* Then imagine that in your mind you have a pair of brackets like these: [. . .] that you can place around your own reactions. Every time you sense any personal reaction or interpretation to any one of the person's comments, imagine that you put those brackets around it. Mentally and emotionally "pick up" the brackets and your reaction that they contain, and set them aside to deal with later. Then return your attention to the other person's report of their experience. It's not easy to be listening to another person and watching your own mind at the same time. With patience and practice it is a skill that can be learned, and used, when you need it if you're motivated to do so. Even if you don't feel that this is something for you, you might want to experiment with it a few times to discover how you filter other people's comments.

A Down-to-Earth Reading of The Lovers Card

Lovers

A reader who interprets cards in relation to their traditional meanings will talk about them in reference to symbolic meanings that he or she learned while studying them. But a reader who is skilled at drawing out subtle underlying emotions may not discuss much if any of the traditional meaning, and will look at how the card applies to someone's unique situation. A person using the cards in a representational way may mention the traditional meaning of the card in a highly tentative manner that invites their client to accept, reject, or think further about that suggestion. The following example demonstrates reading a card with minimum preconceptions about the client and the "precise," "right," or "only" way to read a card.

A man in his thirties, Philip, comes in to my consulting room for a Tarot session. After spending several minutes looking at the Major Arcana cards that were spread randomly face up on the table, in response to the question, "Which card image feels most important to you?" he pulled "The Lovers," and held it in his hand.

Reader: "Why did you pick this card?" I asked.

Philip: "Because love is what I want more than anything, but it is something I don't have."

Reader: "You don't have anyone to love in your life?"

Philip: "Ma'm, I'm a professional accountant. I'm very good with my work, but not so good with women."

Reader: "How so?"

Philip: "I'm a shy person and I usually take too much time before I can talk openly. Even though I strive to be nice, my communication skill is not so good. I fumble with words and I'm clumsy when I try to discuss my emotions. I'm just stuck. I don't know what to do and as much as I try, I'm unable to find a partner.

Reader: "How does that make you feel?"

Philip: "Horrible, like I'm a failure. My love life sucks! I have no emotional stability. I only see problems and more problems. When I reach out, I'm rejected. I feel alone and lonely. I'm fed up with my life."

Reader: I thought I heard silent tears beneath his words. "You sound very sad."

Philip: "Yes. All my efforts end in failure. And now, even if I see an opportunity, I'm afraid of still another rejection. So there is no way for me to be happy. I think your card The Lovers is a lie."

In this representational reading, I let the client tell what meanings he found in his chosen card before I made any comments. That made his burst of painful emotions, his subjective reality, the starting point for our work. There was less danger of upsetting him by jumping to a mistaken conclusion that The Lovers card should have a happy, romantic ending. Because the starting point is the client looking directly at the images and then making his own selection of meaningful cards before disclosing his thoughts and feelings about them, I was not offering an interpretation based on mistaken assumptions.

The above session demonstrates a very different approach than that of a reader who says, "They are paying good money to hear about what I see in their cards. If there's time, they can ask me questions after I give my reading."

At this point you might be thinking: "I'm a reader and I love to talk about the meanings of the cards." This is true for most Tarot enthusiasts, but suspending your own viewpoint and reactions, and responding from as neutral a place as possible can facilitate the client's willingness to voice concerns. Instead of filtering another person's comments through your own card interpretations, you encourage a person to tell their own inner story. There are no "right" or "wrong" answers when someone comments about the images in relation to their personal reality.

Few of us have any idea how much we filter other people's comments through our own interpretations. Listening to someone without translating their world into our own reality is something most of us can profit from working on. Then we can offer our own replies, clearly identified as such. This can help the client to feel supported, or to see the situation from another perspective, as appropriate.

Even if you find it useful to offer two or three different interpretations of a card, and wish to mention your reflections about the way a person may experience it, there is value in helping the client also tell their own story and become more responsible, self-determining, and inwardly free. In that way they can discover their own personal magic.

Reframing: Constructive Transformation of Counterproductive Self-Talk

Magician

Dr. Aaron Beck recognized the importance of shifting negative thought patterns into a more positive direction in order to alleviate suffering and anxiety. He discovered that when his clients were talking to him, often they were also having a silent internal dialogue with themselves. He began asking them to listen to what they were telling themselves while talking out loud to him. This resulted in identifying silent, self-critical mental and verbal patterns. Once they were acknowledged, he worked with the person to find other statements that were both more helpful and more realistic.[2]

This process is now known as reframing (or in more academic phrasing, "cognitive restructuring"). Usually when people utter positive affirmations, they have previously noticed a negative thought or inclination and replaced it with a more optimistic—and hopefully more realistic—one. To better understand this, think about one thought in your mind that tells you, "I can't do that," or "I'm not creative," or whatever you've heard yourself negatively affirm. Once you have such a statement in mind, reframe it by putting your words into a more positive framework. For instance, if I've heard myself saying inward,

"I'm always wasting my energy and never getting things done," I will remind myself to turn that statement into a positive affirmation. You might look at different ways you can do this, but for this example, we're going to reframe it as, "I'm learning to focus my energy on what is most important to me and being more optimistic about reaching my goals."

Now, to further our understanding of reframing, let's bring Philip, who entered our story further back, back into the limelight. He was saying,

Philip: "I think your card, The Lovers, is a lie."

At that point a reader might say something like: "Maybe you can look more at what's good in your life. What can you do to feel better about yourself if you aren't finding love at this time?" (A depth-oriented psychotherapist would probably initiate a more time-consuming exploration of Philip's self-sabotage and its history.)

Philip: "I just don't know. I make the same mistakes again and again."

Reader: "Because words affect actions you might want to change the way you talk to yourself. For example, instead of emphasizing that when you reach for love, it ends in failure, you can look at the courage you have to reach out for love despite your repeated disappointments. Let's look at whether you can transform your unhelpful words into more effective expressions. Can you think of any way to look at your mistakes as stepping stones to successful communication?"

Philip *(looking doubtful)*: "For instance?"

Reader: "You've told me that when you invite a woman to dinner or the movies she usually turns you down."

Philip: " Not 'usually'—always."

Reader: "Perhaps, you're asking for a large commitment of involvement without going through the preliminary steps that would make her more likely to accept."

Philip: "Such as?"

Reader: "If you're at work or school, an invitation for a cup of coffee is a smaller request that's more likely to be accepted. Take some time for chit-chat with the woman you want to date and see if it turns into interesting conversation. If you and she can build something of a friendship, you'll feel more confident and you're less likely to be rejected."

Philip: "That does sound a bit easier. Then what?"

Reader: "If you have coffee together and she seems to enjoy your company, you can go a step farther and invite her to lunch, or a drink after work before heading home."

Philip: "Those are definitely smaller and easier steps."

Reader: "They are. If you don't feel intimidated, you're more likely to project an inviting attitude. And even if you're neutral minded instead of expecting a 'No,' you'll have a better sense of what you can make happen. By contrast, if you're telling yourself that you'll probably be turned down again, you probably will."

Philip: "That sounds sensible. It appeals to a logical person like myself."

Reader: "And you'll want to extend your invitations only when her verbal clues and body language are telling you that she may accept."

Philip: "So it's a matter of taking small steps that even a klutz like me can handle."

Reader: "Exactly. Take a series of small steps rather than one big one. Not everyone has to do that, but with your history of stumbling on a big step, I think you'll find it helpful. And pay attention each time you put yourself down like you did just now."

Philip: "Huh? How did I put myself down?"

Reader: "I think your line was, ' . . even a klutz like me.' That attitude doesn't help. If you tell yourself that you're a klutz, you'll probably act like one. Let's reframe that sentence. Repeat after me: "So it's a matter of taking small steps that a thoughtful, considerate person like me can take.""

Philip: "Okay. It's a matter of taking small steps that a thoughtful, considerate person like me can take." Philip laughs. "Okay. I feel different saying that.""

Reader: (Smiles) "I think you're getting the idea. And this method might help your social skills in other kinds of situations too."

Philip's behavior won't change overnight. He'll need practice and perseverance. At least for now he can see a direction to move that offers a ray of hope.

The "Here and Now"

To read the cards well, you need to see and hear what the person is saying and doing, and respond to their feelings. You also need to notice what you yourself are doing. This means keeping your mind focused on his or her—and your—present behavior in each moment, *even when you're talking about the there-and-then.* It's okay for a person to describe memories of the past or fantasies about the future, but the big benefit comes with keeping the focus on present thoughts, feelings, sensations, and inclinations toward action during such remembering or imagining.

We are not suggesting that you stop your querent or client from talking about the past or future or distant places. Rather, we mean that it's important to ask the person to describe their present experience regarding those events of other times and places. For example, "As I think about the way she walked out on me I feel my stomach and shoulders tightening into knots. I feel my emotional vulnerability and imagine myself as a dead leaf that could be blown away by the slightest wind." When the person drifts into "storytelling" about past, future, or elsewhere, you can gently bring them back: "What are you experiencing right now in your mind and feelings and body?" Or, "What inclination is going through your mind?" In doing this, you are helping the person learn to be present in each moment.

From a Judgmental Attitude to Acceptance and Kindness

Judgment

Few things interfere with being fully present in the now more than a judgmental attitude. When you feel "Here comes da judge," welling up inside you, look out! With such an outlook, you know what's right and wrong for the other person. You know what they ought to do and that if they would just do as you tell them, they'd be fine.

Again, noticing what you're doing in the present moment is the key, and this especially includes noticing when you're manufacturing or hanging on to any judgment, whether your own or those of others.

One of the twentieth century's great psychologists, Carl Rogers, did his best to practice what he termed *unconditional positive regard* in his therapeutic practice. That may fall a bit short of the "unconditional love" that genuine saints and great gurus preach, but it's a long hard road to become a saint or great guru. Rogers meant that he did all he could to fully accept each client exactly as they were when they came to see him, even when others condemned their attitudes or actions.

Adopting the outlook that Rogers modeled and applying it in your own readings or therapy sessions makes people more likely to open up and discuss private feelings, and that usually makes their sessions more valuable. When working to develop a nonjudgmental attitude toward others, a key principle is to apply the same principle of being nonjudgmental to yourself. So if you find yourself feeling judgmental or condemning something in a client, do your best to "step behind your thoughts" and notice yourself being judgmental without putting yourself down for it. Just, "Oh, I'm doing that again right now!" This approach can help you move toward being more accepting of both yourself and others. (It is also part of the meditative practice called "mindfulness" in Buddhist tradition and "witness consciousness" in yogic tradition.)

King of Cups

The Slippery Matter of Ego

A problem with the aspect of ego that's related to self-esteem can afflict both counseling and therapy trainees and novice card readers. Uncertain about their skills, the questions, "Am I doing it right?" or "Am I missing something crucial?" dominate their thinking. Little attention remains for clues that tell what's actually going on with the client. This can be a self-fulfilling prophecy: "Worrying that I am working incorrectly interferes with my ability to work well, and I become more likely to do poor work."

Victor recalls a workshop with Miriam Polster, a leader in his professional community, when he had already been doing gestalt work for more than ten years. He and two other trainees were at one end of a hotel room and Victor was in the therapist's role in the middle of a session. The door to the hallway opened and Miriam came to observe. She sat down near the door, directly in Victor's line of sight. With a direct view of her, suddenly concern about what she was thinking about his work filled his mind and he lost focus. After several minutes of being distracted by Mr. Ego, he turned his chair around so that he could no longer see Miriam and could place his attention completely on the client. Worry about how he was doing diminished and he finished the session doing well.

In short, the psychotherapist or card reader who is committed to voicing only correct interpretations or is worried about performance end up in the same place. Instead of attending to the client's concerns, thoughts, feelings, and actions, so much of their mind is concerned with their need to be right that they have less attention available to work effectively. To work well, you need most of your attention available to the demands and opportunities of each moment. If you think ego isn't very important, recall a recent argument between you and someone else. Most likely it involved a power struggle. It might have been about one person's desire to "be right," or about who makes a decision. At least three-fourths of all arguments are power struggles in which the real issue is that both people want to "win." Instead, both lose. The relationship deteriorates.

Try this: Next time you find yourself in an argument, especially with someone close to you, ask your physical body—"Is the apparent issue what's really at stake here, or is this about who wins?" If the answer is "who wins?" Then you can choose to let go of that concern. And there's a good chance your life will be lighter and brighter than when you struggled to have the last word.

The "Shadows of Sigmund" Spread

Chariot

The "I," in Freud's terms, which A. A. Brill, his first influential translator into English, called "ego," mediates among our basic needs, our desires, and external reality. It's a sort of control center for the "reality-testing," "executive" aspect of the personality that helps a person function in the world.

Now get your deck ready for the following Shadows of Sigmund three-card spread. Here you can choose images from either a face-up or face-down deck.

Pick three cards and place them in a horizontal row starting with the first card on the left and the last one on the right.

Card 1: The "It," in English, often mistranslated as "Id." The Underlying Foundation of Your Being

This card is the foundation for understanding what nurtures your sense of self. "What are my basic needs? How do I, or how can I best take care of them? What do I need to be content?"

Card 2: The "I." The Conscious Center or Core of Your Being (often mistranslated as "Ego.")

This card sits in the center of this spread and represents how you do and don't take care of your psyche. It balances how you respond to the needs associated with the core of your being against your soulful dreams of what or who you are becoming. How do you see yourself?

Card 3: *The "Over-I." Full Moon of The Self (often mistranslated as "superego").*

Where Freud wrote "soul" in German, translator A. A. Brill consistently rendered it as "mind" in English. Some difference! Let's return to Freud's meaning and the expression, "Have you got soul?" and then expand it. What decisions feed your passion? What feels best about your present sense of self? What decisions are you making to help you fulfill your dreams for realizing your highest good? How are you feeding or not feeding your higher spirit, and if you're not, how can you?

Now look at your entire spread. The "It" that reflects your needs, the "I" that addresses how to meet them and more, and the "Over-I" that illuminates the best in your life and your highest hopes. Does any message jump out from your spread, or perhaps peer through the cracks between the cards?

Neon Arrows, Momentum, and Energy

Ace of Pentacles

Another important insight from Victor's workshop with Myriam Polster came from her statement, "That was an excellent session except for one thing. You had both parents in the empty chairs, you were working with the client's relationship with his mother, and near the end of the session the client's energy moved to the father. You were trying to wrap up all the details with the mother when it was time to let go of her and work with Dad."

In other words, "Follow the energy." In therapy, counseling, personal coaching, or reading, the same message holds true: Pay attention to the momentum, to the person's flow of energy, and go with it.

Miriam's husband Erv, one of the most penetrating thinkers in the history of modern gestalt therapy, framed the matter more broadly with his concept of "neon arrows." These metaphoric flaming arrows declare, "Look, this is the dominant flow of energy. This is where you need to work." A neon arrow may be a quiver or break in the voice. It may be a brief mention of an incident before quickly jumping to something else.

It may be a physical gesture that says something the person's words don't, or an unusual use of words that seem somehow out of place. It may be tears forming in the corner of an eye that do not quite roll down the cheek. It may be finishing with one card or issue while an almost-hidden clue suggests that something else is about to burst through a dam of pent up emotions.

You can't learn sensitivity to the spectrum of these neon arrows from a book. It is an intuitive capacity that some people naturally possess to a greater or lesser degree, and that others can develop through working with many people over an extended period. Be alert for such cues and clues. But if you think you're following one, yet it isn't and you're not, forget it. Time will soon let you know if another is pointing in a different direction. Like a dowser looking for water, watch and listen for those neon arrows that can tell you where the hidden energy is flowing.

Part of a psychotherapist's, counselor's, or reader's job is to help their clients become better at handling the varied kinds of energy in their minds, emotions, and bodies. Sadly, at times everybody has to cope with obstacles, difficulties, or loss. Occasionally these can be extreme. Physical energy experts Amory and Hunter Lovins speak of *brittle* and *resilient* systems. A brittle system breaks down more easily and is harder to repair. A resilient system stands up better in the face of stress and recovers more easily when problems occur.[4]

These concepts also apply to our personalities. Effective work will soften the hard edges of a client's brittle ways of handling challenges and help them develop coping strategies that are more resilient. In turn, that leads toward a more cheerful attitude. It brings a stronger, deeper sense of self. When a person has been through a traumatic experience, it can be challenging to find a way to soften the harsh edges of reality—but even then, it is possible to offer guidance leading to hope and recovery. On the other hand, sometimes even a ten-minute "quick" reading can offer one personal tool that a person can use to raise their resilience and improve their state of mind.

Perhaps you or the other person may be functioning well, but have a sense of something missing, something deeper. Some cards point to moving beyond our usual everyday outlooks toward a fuller connection with other people, and even with our own self. Such an attitude involves connecting with the deepest and highest dimensions of your spiritual self (which may or may not be connected with any organized religion).

That path leads beyond "fix my problems" into the realm that psychologists call "transpersonal." Reading the cards with such a purpose can explicitly awaken an evolutionary sense of self and take people in transcendent directions. "Your vision will become clear only when you look into your heart. Who looks outside dreams. Who looks inside awakens," said Carl Jung.[5]

Until now, everything written here has been about working with one person at a time. We have not gone into the dynamics of working in a small group of people, with participation by all who are present, or with a couple in a session where both are present. All that comes next.

3 *of* WATERS

PART III

Further Travels on a Novel Path

10.

TAROT GROUPS

Groups can offer a panoramic kaleidoscope to see into other people's lives. They provide structure, support, multiple perspectives, and knowledge to uplift or educate those interrelated by beliefs, needs, or parallel problems. There are numerous private interest organizations, such as gestalt groups for healing emotions, Tantric groups for improving one's love life, and various associations for help controlling addictions. Some people come together in brainstorming encounters where their identical purpose is motivating lofty levels of financial success. Also, there are spiritual groups and various meditation, metaphysical, and Tarot groups where inquiring minds come together to accelerate learning and build community.

At various times, we have participated in many different groups, both as participants and as leaders. One of our favorite groups was a dream-sharing group developed by our colleague, mentor, and charismatic Jungian psychologist, Gordon Tappan. Several years ago it occurred to us that with minor adjustments, Tappan's style of dream groups could be adapted for use with the Tarot. We tried it and it worked seamlessly for a Tarot group reading. We offer it here for those of you who would like to learn this process and offer others the opportunity to take part in a similar experience.

If your interest in the Tarot persists over time, sooner or later you're likely to find yourself at a gathering surrounded by other Tarot enthusiasts. Such a time or when you're with friends interested in the Tarot, or if you are doing a workshop or a conference session, or even leading a process group composed of people who know nothing about the Tarot, you can initiate such an experience.

The outcome of several people doing the Tarot together always contains surprises. Often it's a time to summon and receive meaningful insights and wisdom that benefit all. The best size for such a group is three to twelve participants, including the leader, although with co-facilitators, a group of twenty people is manageable—(but time allowed for participants to share insights is not ideal). Whatever the group size, let your creativity flow and spontaneously follow the energy of the moment. Whether you're a novice or a pro, you can make such an interactive reading a powerful event.

Creating and Facilitating a Tarot Group

First participants form themselves into a small circle, either sitting around a table or on cushions or the floor. One person volunteers to be the person who receives the reading. He or she might state a specific concern, hold a question silently in mind, or merely be curious about whatever insights will emerge.

While you give instructions for this process, shuffle your cards and set the deck in the center of the group. Encourage the person who will be getting the reading to think about their life situation, question, or concerns. Then ask this person to draw a specific number of cards and hand them to you. (You have the option of asking a person to choose from face-down or face-up cards, or of leaving that choice to him or her.) Hold each card up, identify it by name, and place it face up in the middle of the table or floor so that everyone can see them all.

As group facilitator, you can place the cards in whatever spread you prefer. In a therapy group designed for working through thoughts and feelings about a recent or past trauma, for example, you might design a spread specifically appropriate to that goal. (Yes, it's up to you to determine which spread best meets the needs of the situation and the moment.) We often use the following seven-card spread called The Mind-Heart Connection since it has wide potential applications.

The "Mind-Heart Connection Spread"

This spread provides an opportunity to look deeply into a person's thoughts and feelings in relation to his or her concerns and questions. The guidelines for laying the cards in this spread are straightforward. Cards one, two, and three, in the top horizontal row, are linked with the

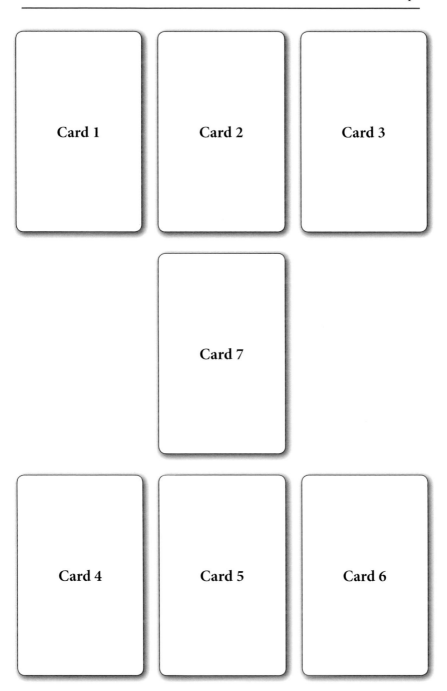

querent's mind and ideas about his or her situation. Cards four, five, and six, in the bottom horizontal row, are linked with the querent's emotions and feelings about his or her situation. The seventh card placed in the middle of the two rows, is comparable to a ladder that allows a person to go up and down from one row to the other in relation to the head and heart's combined direction.

Card 1: *The situation.*
What is this person's concern?

Card 2: *The question.*
Can the main issues be stated as a question that is relevant to others in the circle? Do others have similar concerns or thoughts?

Card 3: *Opportunities.*
What possibilities can expand the positive options in the querent's situation? Are there ideas for change or improvement?

Card 4: *Hopes and Fears.*
What is the person afraid of, hopeful about, or both? What is she or he sensing?

Card 5: *Hidden Strength(s).*
What less-than-obvious feelings and abilities does the person possess that can help in this situation?

Card 6: *Under-used capacity(ies).*
What neglected ability or abilities can he or she develop to handle the situation more effectively? What is his or her heart sense in regards to taking action?

Card 7: *A positive direction.*
Starting from here, what kind of path does the person want to traverse in this matter? How does this card address the issue in relation to combining feelings and ideas?

The Structure of Our Tarot Group Process

After the cards are placed in the spread, there is a go-around in which each person in the circle has several minutes to talk about their impressions or gut reaction to the images on the cards.

It is good to let people know that they are not expected to be "readers" of the cards, nor are they are expected to have studied Tarot interpretation. Also, when you invite everyone to participate in the discussion, explicitly tell them that there isn't any right or wrong idea relating to what they feel about an image, so that they will be more comfortable discussing what they see in the cards. Each person can respond to others' comments only after everyone in the circle has had a turn discussing what the spread means to them personally. In other words, ask people not to interrupt whoever is commenting on the cards.

A key point: No one should presume to know anything about the meaning of the spread for the client but should "own" the personal meanings he or she finds in the card. You may ask each person to start with the phrase: "This is how the spread applies to me." Or "*If this were my reading, what I make of it for myself is . . .*" This practice leaves the querent free to think, "Yes, that meaning fits for me," or "No, that may be true for that person but not for me." Inevitably, some other group members' reactions hit home with the querent or client while others don't. Still, some of those who don't are likely to be relevant for others in the group.

This procedure nips "I know what's going on with you" assumptions in the bud. Such assumptions, and also intellectualizing about the card meanings rather than offering personal responses, are quick ways to deaden or kill the process. Also, its good to ask that while one person is speaking, no one interrupts except perhaps to ask a clarifying question when someone didn't hear or understand something.

After one person has responded to the spread, the next person in the circle repeats the process until everyone in the circle has had a turn. The person who is commenting can respond as he or she pleases, whether this involves the card's traditional meanings, uniquely personal replies, or anything that ignites his or her impressions at that moment.

Depending on the number of participants, a time limit may be placed on each person's statement. One person can monitor the time so that no one rambles on too long, taking away others' opportunities to speak. Or a watch can be passed around with the person next to each speaker keeping track of time for the speaker. The time allowed for each person in a large group may be as little as three or four minutes, or in a small group as many as ten minutes. It's okay for a person to use less than their time allowance, or to say something like "I'll pass" and say nothing. Typically, the entire group reading should take no more than an hour.

After everyone who wishes has spoken in the go-around, you as the group facilitator turn to the querent or client and ask, "What did others say that rings true for you?" The person replies with their personal experience of having listened to everyone's comments.

Then, if time permits, in your role as leader you have the option to continue by offering a "public" reading of the spread. If you're doing a reading rather than therapy, you may want to summarize your understanding of what the cards represent and offer a few words about their traditional significance. Possibly you will feel inclined to describe them in relation to what they personally mean to you. Then you might choose to open the circle to a discussion in which each group member may make one last brief remark. It may contain several comments, but then the person stops so that others get a turn. Everyone has the option of talking privately with the querent or client later.

Consider two basic ground rules to promote a harmonious conclusion of your work:

1. Such final comments MAY NOT be interpretations or intellectualizations. Rather, they are each group member's personal statement of their own feelings. This reduces the chances of obvious or disguised critical-minded finger pointing, and contributes to closure. Here too, each member may speak or not.

2. During such a process each person may speak only about his or her own feelings, thoughts, or other reactions. No one may speak for any other member of the group, such as in the comment, "Well, I think most people here feel . . . " If anyone violates this fundamental rule and makes such a comment, the group leader gently intervenes with a comment such as "Please do not speak for others. We can certainly hear just a sentence from each person about how *they themselves actually do* feel right now." Usually there is a wide spectrum of feelings and thoughts among group members, and the person making the "I think others feel . . . " comment was projecting his or her own reactions onto others.

We thank Carl Rogers for emphasizing this principle of "Speak from your own personal frame of reference" rather than making judgments or assumptions about how others are reacting. It does away with a huge number of arguments and mistaken notions. You and I can argue all day about what is or isn't so, but when you tell me *what you personally think and feel about something*, you're the ultimate authority and I have no grounds to contradict you—and vice-versa.

The total time available for the group work, the number of participants, and how long the process just described takes, are factors that influence whether there is only one "group reading" or whether there is time for two or even several. If the group is quite small or the time is long, then everyone might have a chance to take a turn being a querent, client, or leader.

If this process "goes too deep" for any group member and he or she feels shaky at the end of it, another group member or the leader can offer support until they feel "on solid ground" again. Sharing positive energy usually helps a person feel emotionally grounded and more receptive to relaxing in the moment.

In your Tarot circle, you need two essential agreements, "confidentiality" and "no gossiping." "Confidentiality" means that before the process begins, in order to participate each member must agree that anything revealed by any person during the group process or the reading "stays within the room" and will not be disclosed to anyone who is not in the group. In no way should any person's words or actions be discussed or identified to anyone outside the group. "No gossiping" means that group members do not talk with each other inside or outside the group about what other group members said and did during it.

At the beginning of a group, we like to have a mini-ceremony in which all members stand in a circle and hold hands to symbolize agreement to these two principles. Anyone who is unwilling to agree to them should leave the group.

We have concluded that what occurs during this kind of group process depends on:

1. The cards that were selected,
2. The detailed observations by the querent or client and best guesses about which of a card's various meanings are relevant for him or her,
3. Other group members' reflections about how the images apply to them personally, and

4. The leader's own background and style of facilitating. The leader's conversation with the client after others have spoken in the go-around can even take the form of identification and projective dialogues if the leader is trained in such work.

Also, if more than an hour is available, a break in the middle of the session often is useful (depending on how the energy is flowing). Or there can be an agreement that any person can quietly and unobtrusively leave to take care of their personal needs.

Exploring the Life-Space in a Group

Mentioned earlier in Chapter 3, the Life-Space Card Spread is also useful in groups. It lends itself to sharing feelings and insightful interactions with people who might be more comfortable talking publicly about their life through the medium of the cards than without them. We'll recap the instructions for working with this spread here and include the group element.

If your group does not have Tarot cards, you will need to supply a number of decks for people to use. Or you can place one or more decks of face-up cards in the middle of the working space and have everyone share cards from which to choose images for their own use.

To expand on instructions given in Chapter 3, each person receives a very large piece of paper, such as a sheet of butcher or art paper and a handful of different colored marking pens or crayons. (A pile of marking pens for several people who are sitting near each other will do.) Participants spread their sheets of paper on tables or the floor. Then they quickly make a drawing of all the physical places they visit in the course of their daily lives. Thick lines reflect places where they often go, while narrow lines reflect the places they only occasionally go. Roads and buildings are likely to be prominent features. For people who have a hard time drawing, you can ask them to simply draw the best they can. No one should judge anyone's stick figure representations.

Wherever someone who is significant to the querent or client is found, a card is chosen for that person and placed where it belongs on the "life-space map." (A location might have two cards to represent two or more people, such as in the home or office). Also, have the person put a star by any card where he or she feels an emotional charge. A card can also be chosen for a place (rather than a person) that has some kind of feeling or special memory or meaning attached to it. Much of the sheet of paper will probably be taken up by places the person visits in daily life, with no card attached. A hardware store or beauty parlor might be on the map due to frequent visits, but have no card. The rest of the sheet, around the outside edges, is used for dotted lines to mark places far away that are important for some reason, or places the person has been or lived in the past but seldom or never visits now.

The Life-Space Card Spread should include a card for one's neighborhood, the workplace, personal space, and co-workers or home and family depending on who is your primary focus while doing this exercise. A workplace or school might have just a dot or a card, or might include several different buildings or offices, some with cards and some without. Twenty minutes or less is a reasonable time to allow for this.

If a person works in an organization, his or her life-space map might be focused on places and events within it. But some participants might mention outside places and interests that open up different possibilities for how they see their life-space.

Once the life-space map is drawn, each person takes a few minutes to tell other group members about his or her map and respond to questions. If the group is larger than about eight people, you can break it into two or more smaller groups for the discussion period. Then after discussing their Life Spread in the smaller group, any strong feelings or deep insights that have emerged can be shared with the entire group if a person wishes to do so. (Anyone who does not feel secure discussing their feelings and ideas with the group has the option of giving a superficial interpretation of their cards and reactions, to protect sensitive emotions.)

When time is tight, participants can divide into pairs and describe their life-space map just to one partner. This process can be useful for opening up communication between members of a work group or organization who seldom interact with each other, by asking participants to choose people they do not know well as partners. This can open new avenues of communication, collaboration, and creativity.

Tarot Group Problem Solving

When several or more people are involved in some matter, you and the Tarot can all come together to bring clarity to the group concern. First have your circle of friends or colleagues state their intention for the gathering and the key item for discussion. Then the facilitator shuffles the cards, fans them out face down, and asks each person in the circle to select one card for insight gathering.

The images on each person's chosen card can be discussed either by the person who has picked the card or by anyone who has a comment about the images in relation to the group question. Discussing images can be a nonthreatening way to get people to talk about ideas or suggest possibilities. Sometimes unanticipated comments surprise everyone and trigger an avalanche of new possibilities, but the facilitator should keep the conversation focused within the context of the group question and ensure that everyone has approximately equal speaking time. If a few big-time talkers are monopolizing the discussion, this can be done with an intervention such as, "To give everyone a chance for input, for the next fifteen minutes let's hear only from people who have not yet spoken."

If you're the facilitator, you can encourage dialogue with questions such as, "What message does this image hold for you?" or "What, if anything, is triggered in you by this image that can add insight to our situation? or "Does this image point toward anything positive, or a potential resolution?" A light-hearted approach can encourage thought-provoking discussions and move toward transformative results.

If the goal is creative problem solving, it's helpful to divide the session into two parts. During the first part, "brainstorming," all criticism, critique, or judgment of anyone's suggestion, no matter how bizarre it may be, is off limits. This opens people up to being comfortable and more willing to reveal their ideas. During the second part, "evaluation and improvement," people can point out a problem with a suggestion made during the brainstorming period, and whenever possible, suggest an improvement that may make a questionable solution work. A card that they themselves or someone else drew may point to such a possible improvement or suggest a new perspective in relation to the same image.

During either "brainstorming" or "evaluation and improvement," anyone can reach into the pile of cards and draw one or more new ones that might shake up their thoughts or the conversation.

Reading for Couples

Imagery can also be used for reading or counseling much smaller groups, including the smallest of all, the couple. You can expect the unexpected—and also variations on dynamics you've seen played out many times before. Whether the couple is one in a romantic or business partnership, such sessions require complete focus. Depending on the emotional state of the couple, and the issue(s) they bring up, this can be quite demanding of your ability to remain an objective bystander who is open hearted, empathic, and able to provide healing arbitration. Attempt couples reading only if you are completely comfortable doing multifaceted Tarot readings or are a skilled couples counselor.

Here we describe two spreads for use with couples. (Of course, you are free to choose any spread you think is most appropriate. Couples can also be mother-daughter, husband-wife, husband-mistress, or whoever makes a couple).

First we look at a six-card past-present-future spread, to represent the past or foundation of the couple's concerns, the present feelings in this moment, and potential future possibilities. The cards on the bottom represent the past; the cards in the middle, the present, and the two cards on the top indicate the future potential.

The couple begins by deciding whether they want to use the cards in a representational or divinatory manner. Do they want a general reading or do they have a specific question or issue as their focus? For now, let's imagine that you're going to do a divinatory reading for a general question and your couple has completed their card shuffle. Let each person have a turn at cutting the deck into two stacks and putting them face down on the table. Ask each person to choose one of the stacks to answer his or her own questions during the reading. Then turn over the top three cards in each person's chosen stack. Place each person's three cards face up in a vertical column that is parallel his or her partner's vertical row of three cards. When you look at the couple's card layout, it looks like a six-card spread made of two vertical columns of three cards each.

Once all six cards are on the table, you will want to discuss the cards in relation to each pair that represents past, present, or future. Let's suppose that you are doing a reading for a man and a woman who are considering marriage. First, look at both cards positioned on the bottom of the two columns that represent the past. What does each image convey? For example, if one card is The Sun linked with positive energy, and the other card is the Six of Cups that represents sharing happy emotions, you might interpret this to mean that their past can support a happy union. But if one card is the Hanged Man and one is the Six of Pentacles, you might consider asking the couple if they are prepared for the financial responsibilities of joining their lives together, or if they have mutually agreeable financial expectations. If the stated purpose of the reading is compatibility, you want to understand what each pair of cards represents to the couple. What do they each feel when comparing images on the lower two cards that represent the past, or the middle two cards that represent the present, or the two in the top row linked with the future? If you draw out each person's thoughts and feelings as they look at the cards, the chemistry between the couple, and how they share energy will begin to emerge—often very quickly. Whether the symbolism on the chosen cards offers vivid clues about the couple or not, the couple's ways of communicating will offer insight into their relationship. (For example, we remember one couple in which neither person could speak a sentence without the other person interrupting and arguing with it.)

An alternative to designating the three cards in each column as past, present, and future is to ask which aspects of their relationship they're most concerned about. Then use that information to label the positions of the cards in direct response to their concerns. An example of creating card positions in relations to specific questions might involve one pair of cards being designated as "Relationships with partner's family," another designated "Values in saving and spending," and a third labeled "Children or no children? Or "Where should we live?" The couple's concerns determine the card positions and the direction the conversation goes.

After you are experienced and comfortable doing six card couples' readings, you can draw more cards for each person. We find drawing seven cards for each person and placing them in parallel vertical columns to create a fourteen-card spread, provide a bountiful opportunity for discussion. Each pair of cards from the two partners can represent a different topic. Or alternatively, topics for the positions may not be specified, with the comparison between each pair of cards left open-ended, to see what emerges.

Also, if time permits, additional cards that create emotional stacks can be added when appropriate. However, since such readings become more complex, more time discussing cards and relationship dynamics is needed.

Opening the reading to emotional stacks can throw unexpected "wild cards" into the reading. It can open new ways of thinking about a dilemma and sometimes bring a change in behavior, (Note: Adding additional emotional stacks in a couple's reading can make your work appear more insightful, but it isn't necessarily easy.)

If you are doing a representational reading and the couple has drawn their cards from a face-up deck, you will let the images they select be the focus of their reading. You may still want to consider the underlying question or concern, but you will let the couple's discussion of why they chose specific images be more central than your comments about the position of the cards and how pairs of cards interface with one another.

If the cards being chosen bring up difficulties, you may want to let their conversation continue until you sense that it is time to select a "wisdom card" or "wise advisor" or "fairy godmother" card (See Chapter 7) whose image can offer a mutually acceptable understanding or positive resolution to the discussion that can lead to closure of your work.

Right now if you can, from your deck take out one of your favorite cards that makes you feel good. Breathe into this image and let your spirit feel excited with the prospects of using your cards, or using them in new ways. The more you work with couples and/or groups, the easier it will become to understand and develop effective card methods for successful interactions. Now before we put on our safety belt and descend toward inner space, we'll say adieu to group and couples work. In coming pages, we offer a few words about how meditation can be useful in the context of the Tarot.

11.
—

MEDITATION AND THE TAROT

Inwardly Connecting with a Card or Image

Meditation is ". . . A systematic technique for taking hold of and concentrating to the utmost degree our latent mental power…so that we can set forth from the surface level of consciousness and journey into the very depths," declared Eknath Easwaran, founder of the Blue Mountain Meditation Center.[1]

We can all benefit from quieting the mind, but many of the advantages of combining Tarot and meditation can only be truly known through direct experience. When someone talks about "meditating on the cards," usually they're referring to focusing their thoughts on the possible meanings in a card or cards. But developing a meditative focus and becoming "one" with a card or other image allows us to expand our understanding and recognize its meaning on a deeper level.

Recently the scientific as well as the spiritual community has documented positive results of meditation, including effects on heart rate, blood pressure, and physical tension, as well as those on our mind and emotions. The real proof of its value, however, comes when we experience its benefits on a personal level. If your time permits, we'd like to begin with a contemplative meditation on just one card to inwardly connect with its essence. Please allow yourself at least five minutes to do the following awareness exercise to become better acquainted with a card's meaning and implications.

First, get out your favorite deck of cards and select a card of your choice. Look at it intently with your eyes wide open for as long as you wish. Then close your eyes. Breathe deeply, and with your mind's inward eye see yourself merging with the primary image in the card.

- What is he or she thinking? Become the voice for this image.
- What does he, she, or it want to say?
- How does your body react and move?
- What does your inner guide tell you to do in relation to connecting with the essence of this card?
- Does this card have a personal message for you? If so, how can you put it into practice?

Other Forms of Meditation

Creating a mentally and emotionally supportive sanctuary where you block out the demands of the world and focus completely on the present moment is a first step toward meditation. This doesn't have to be in a church or a forest. It can be in your own backyard or living room.

Quiet, reflective contemplation about something important to you is just one form of meditation. For many centuries it was the only meaning of the word understood by most people in the West. As communication around the globe has increased, other methods rooted in Yogic, Buddhist, and Taoist traditions have migrated westward and now play vital roles in many people's lives. Although there are many meditative paths, here we discuss just five. Our primary focus is on their use with card imagery. The five are:

1. Concentration

This is developing mind control—especially the ability to focus your attention and be aware of what your thoughts are doing at a given moment. When doing a reading, focusing on your client and his or her interactions with the cards helps you to tune out everyone and everything that is not in your immediate space. With sword-point focus, you can give your entire attention to being with the client, and when your mind wanders, bring it back from distractions to refocus on the person and cards.

2. Mindfulness

(Buddhist label) or *witness consciousness* (Yogic label) is sometimes called "two pointed attention." This requires a focused inner awareness of noticing the flow of what your thoughts, emotions, and body are doing moment by moment as if you were an observer watching yourself. Some teachers also apply these terms to noticing whatever is going on outside you in your physical environment. When you sharpen your awareness of what is happening inside and outside of yourself, you enhance your ability to be present to your client's needs.

3. Everyday awareness practices
These include methods for consciously taking meditative awareness into your practical or worldly daily life. This also helps you develop focused attention in the present moment.

4. Stress-reduction meditation
This involves applying everyday awareness practices in emergency situations when your person is "freaking out" or "losing it." Your central task during such a time, is to be calm, reassuring, and aware as you deliver healing energies and techniques that will support and knit together fraying emotions. This can enable someone to get through their reactions to challenging events and make it safely "home"—literally or figuratively.

5. Contemplative meditation
This method entails systematic reflection and examination of one's life and personal history. It promotes greater personal awareness and insight by illuminating inner truth as it dispels the fog of distorted misperceptions. Only when someone recognizes self-defeating patterns can they develop more effective ones.

From Concentrative to Contemplative Meditation

Centering, breathing, focusing, and witnessing the mind are meditative elements used to penetrate deeper levels of consciousness. When reflecting on card images, your own personal associations with them can open the floodgates of your stream-of-consciousness, your transcendental passage to whatever thoughts, feelings, memories, sensations, or inclinations spontaneously emerge. Some of these may bubble up from your unconscious without your having previous knowledge that they were part of you, bypassing the logical thinking about an image or memorizing a scholarly card interpretation that can keep a lid on deeper feelings, sensations, or associations related to it.

How, then, do you "contemplate without thinking?" The key is to go into a calm, receptive, non-critical state of consciousness rather than a conceptual problem-solving mode of thinking, which is where most of us spend most of our time.

Physical centering, consciously relaxing your breathing, and noticing and releasing muscle tension are first steps in empowering your concentrative and witnessing nature. In turn, these preliminary acts set the stage for contemplative meditation.

Sit up straight, unless it's physically uncomfortable for you to do so. Place any card from your deck *face down* a few feet in front of you. Focus your attention on it as intently as you can. Whenever you notice anything other than the physical image of the back of that card running through your mind, bring your attention back to that face-down card. You're not trying to push anything out of your mind. Rather, you're noticing whatever comes into your mind, and then letting it go rather than letting it monopolize your attention. Then refocus your attention on the card. Doing this helps develop concentration. It's a learnable ability.

You are also learning to be "mindful," to "witness" what your mind is doing. As you become more adept at doing concentrative meditation, you are developing more control over your mental activities. Your mental functioning becomes more efficient and effective. You'll spend less of your mental capacity on items that have no value for you.

If your mind keeps "running away" while you meditate on your face-down card, you may find it useful to use a *moving mudra* (finger yoga) to help you still your mind. Let the thumb and first finger or middle finger of each hand barely touch. Now, as you inhale, let them separate by about a eighth of an inch. As you exhale, let them touch. Repeating this slight finger movement in rhythm with your inhalations and exhalations can help keep your attention focused in the present moment.

Once you have a sense that you are attaining some degree of witnessing your own thoughts, emotional reactions, and sensations, you can turn your card over and use its illustration as an object for your contemplative meditation. If you don't want to focus on this card's image, put it back in the deck and select another. Then put the rest of the deck aside and leave that card in front of you. Do your best to maintain a state of witness consciousness. Breathe consciously, and when any image, thought, memory, hope, sensation, or perspective related to your face-up card occurs to you, stay with it for as long as seems valuable. Then return your attention to the image itself, and wait to notice whatever comes next into your mind.

Such contemplation can even be done with more than one card, but we suggest no more than three, or you're likely to float out of the realm of contemplation into the realm of everyday thinking before you've even noticed. This meditation can help you discover what personal insights the card images may hold for you.

If you are doing a daily contemplative meditation on the Tarot and keeping a Tarot journal, you can take a couple of minutes to jot down the reflections, insights, feelings, sensations, or inclinations that come to you during your meditation. The entry need only be long enough to keep you from forgetting what you experienced or realized. Be sure to give each entry a title, even if only one word, and jot down the card or card's name that it's related to. A title makes it easy to find a specific journal entry at a future time.

If you don't take time for contemplative meditation on a card each day, you might find it useful to have a practice of drawing one card in the morning, and perhaps read its brief entry in the booklet that came with the deck, or its entry in your favorite Tarot book. Then during the day, whenever you remember, you can reflect briefly about whether the card has some message that might be helpful in what you're doing right then.

Meditation Before Starting a Reading

A meditative state of mind allows people to feel fully present and better able to pay attention to what's going on in them and around them Most readers and therapists alike are apt to feel better before, during, and after their sessions if they take time to engage in some kind of meditation before they start their work— even if it's just while shuffling the cards.

Before someone sits down for a reading or counseling session, consider taking a minute or two to do some type of centering meditation. You can close your eyes and tune inward to connect with whatever sensations you feel in your body, whatever pictures appear in your mind, whatever words or phrases come into your head during that brief interval of going into your inner self.

This basic practice serves two purposes. First, it helps you let go of any lingering sensations or impressions from what you were previously doing or whom you were previously with in order to be fully present in the now. Second, it gives you a chance to become fully present with yourself and more aware of the person who will be sitting in front of you. Don't be too surprised if sometimes information comes to you through sensations, or mental pictures, or words that give you clues to what this person needs even before he or she has walked in the door or when they have done no more than say "Hello." Or perhaps a pre-reading meditation will enhance your state of mind or help you to simply relax in the moment and be "all there" with the person, their concerns, and the cards.

Meditations To Begin A Reading

You can also do a mini-meditation at the start of a reading. Carefully arrange the objects on your table and mindfully bring a moment-by-moment focus of awareness to what you are doing. When you notice that your mind is drifting, bring it back to direct visual and tactile awareness of your table and your cards.

You can also use a "focused awareness continuum" meditation to get a first impression of a client or querent. Basically, this is an in-the-moment breathing and focusing practice, while watching the evolving stage of reality from one breath and moment to another. What are you aware of in your present external reality? How does a person come through the door and say hello? What statements do his or her posture, gestures, and tone of voice make? Does he or she initiate or hold back. Often all this can be seen, as you are in the kind of semi-meditative alertness that helped you get mentally ready for the session.

You may also find value in doing your own awareness continuum. "Now I am aware of…." "And now I am aware of …." as you practice conscious breathing while you are shuffling, cutting or laying out cards. This practice enhances mental clarity and prepares you for the coming moment as you and your client, the person sitting across from you, prepare to drink from the universal well of symbolic Tarot wisdom.

Sharpening Mental Focus

Learning to focus our attention can serve as an awareness practice when we remember to practice doing it. Sometimes an occasion arises when it's especially needed. Three elements can make this practice more powerful. First, consciously balance and maintain a stance that is steady and ready for whatever comes from any direction.

We invite you right now, as you read, to take just a few moments to check your physical balance. You can do this sitting or standing. Move your torso slightly forward until you feel off balance in relation to gravity, then back to a more centered feeling. Then move slightly backward until you feel off balance, then forward to your center. Lean right, and then left, and in each case return to the point where you feel most perfectly balanced.

Next, consciously sense your breathing, perhaps for about ten breaths—or longer if that's helpful. If your breathing is short or jerky or irregular, let it become smoother and deeper and more regular.

Finally, let your focus of attention move through your body. Notice anywhere you are holding any muscle tightness not needed for sitting up, and release and let it go. Most people are especially likely to hold tension in the forehead, around the eyes, in the jaw, neck, shoulders, forearms, hands, stomach, butt, calves, and even toes. Don't you sometimes curl your toes during a tense movie?

As you balance, breathe, and release tension, your energy is likely to subtly change and you will probably feel more relaxed and aligned in your body. Also, if you are with someone, he or she may unconsciously mirror your more relaxed state.

Besides using words, you might want to draw a card as a visual image to help remind you to keep your balance. If so, pull the eleventh (in some decks, the eighth) Major Arcana card Justice from your deck and set it where you can see it. Most depictions of this card illustrate a scale of balance that represents weighing positive and negative attributes, maintaining equilibrium, and/or finding inner balance. You can meditate on this card or look at it through your memory to remind you to keep your mental, emotional, and physical balance.

Teaching Basic Meditation Skills

If you have an intuitive sense that your querent needs some minimal meditative grounding to cope with challenging thoughts, emotions, or actions, you can ask, "Do you have any kind of personal meditation practice?" You might describe a way in which one of the cards in the reading points to the need for such a practice, and then take several minutes to teach the person a basic method within the reading.

Why do that? Because meditation is a technique to help a person change whatever is not working in their life, and become more confident when facing a world of stressors. Benefits include:

- Better emotional control
- Being less scattered
- Feeling less stress
- Greater physical, emotional, and mental wellbeing
- Increased mental focus and effectiveness
- Expanded opportunities for self-discovery
- A better quality of relating to others

These benefits don't happen overnight. But after a little effort, meditation usually helps people become more focused, more understanding of inner dilemmas, and more able to listen to their own inner guides.

An Example of a Reading with Stress-Reduction Meditation Instruction

Above we discussed five types of meditation practices. In the unusual situation described below, a person who was having an emotional meltdown in public sat down for a reading. In response, the reader walked her through a calming stress-reduction meditation before proceeding.

At a large, noisy party, a woman in her late twenties whose boyfriend had just ditched her was in the middle of an emotional meltdown, trying to control her sobbing. She could barely speak when she sat down for her reading. The obvious need was to help her get through her sense of panic. It seemed as though a mini-meditation might give her a means to calm herself.

After offering her the basic interventions of centering, focusing, releasing muscle tensions, attending to here-and-now sensory events and replacing unhelpful statements in her mind with suggested positive ones, she began to appear calmer. Since she was emotionally "hanging on by her fingernails," the reader asked:

"Remember the old adage of counting to ten when you're angry before you say or do anything?"

"Yes," she replied.

"This is sort of like that, with a couple of new twists. I want you to count to ten. As you do, pay attention to your breathing, breathe more slowly and deeply, and count one number for each breath. You can close your eyes and try to visualize the number if you like. Say the number to yourself as you inhale, then *empty out all the thoughts and feelings that are rattling around inside your mind as you exhale.* I'll count out loud together with you for the first few breaths, and then you can finish on your own. Okay?"

"S...sh..sure," she said shakily.

"All right. Now inhale deeply and slowly and as you inhale, say ONE. I'll do it together with you." The reader counted out loud with her for five breaths and then fell silent and let her continue by herself. When she got to ten, the reader asked, "Are you with me?"

"Yes, I'm here."

"Now we'll do another ten deep slow breaths. Count from one to ten as you did before, with one difference. Be sure to notice anywhere that you're holding muscle tension in your body, and then as you exhale, release your tension and let that part of your body become as relaxed as possible. With the next breath, find another tense spot and do the same thing. Now go ahead."

By the time she was halfway through her second sequence of ten, the lines in her face were relaxing.

"Now," said the reader, "your goal is to stay as balanced and relaxed as you can. Scan for physical tension and let it go when you feel it. Can you do that?"

"I hope so."

Since the woman was no longer shaking and sobbing, the reader was able to start reading the cards. Whether someone is in a fairly "normal" mental and emotional state, or like this woman who is having a serious problem, providing the most basic meditation tools, gives a person something to put into practice that can help their inner process if they choose to do so.

Meditating on Symbols

Every image on a card is a symbol. It can be a numeric symbol, an archetypal or astrological symbol, a religious or mystical sign, or a metaphorical representation of something valuable or dangerous.

A great way to learn more about symbols is to chose one that charms your curiosity and spend some time meditating on it. For example, if it's cold outside or you feel emotionally blue, you might choose the nineteenth major card, The Sun, from your deck and meditate on its shining image. You can close your eyes and look inward to visualize its golden orb in your mind's eye. Envision its light radiating and expanding throughout your body, warming you inside and out. You might see the Sun as a light within yourself that shines brightly to illuminate your path and perhaps even the paths of others around you, or you might associate it with the Egyptian god Ra, and imagine yourself being initiated into an ancient secret order. Or, possibly it will trigger a memory of a happy moment you spent on a hillside covered with flowers on a sunny day and the image will become a visual reminder that nature can warm your emotions. Let your mind reflect on the possibilities of what the image may mean for you.

Symbols on the cards can also be compared to arrows that point you in the direction of meaningful self-dialogue and/or increased awareness of your own or others' mental processes. Whether you have a scientific, religious, or "neither of the above" approach to viewing symbols, and whether you see pictures and symbols in your dreams or not, when your mind is meditatively quiet, your ability to see beneath the surface is enhanced—like a calm lake or river in contrast to one where the wind is blowing up choppy whitecaps.

Sometimes you'll be able to recognize precisely the images that point to emotional triggers, or those that offer unique personal insights. Or you might even find an image on a card that reminds you of one of your favorite, most comforting places, and then use it to help you bring the good feelings from that distant place into your present.

A Valuable Next Step

This chapter barely scratches the surface of doing a meditative practice with its central focus on the Tarot. As you continue, the true benefits of meditation are likely to enhance your self-discovery in unpredictable and varied ways. But be careful not to make the meditative dimension of the cards into a chore. If you find yourself becoming overly serious, change what you're doing and work with the images in a more light-hearted manner!

When you have a free moment, take your Major Arcana cards out of your deck and put them in their numeric sequence that is shown on the cards, often written in Roman Numerals. You're about to mentally walk into the realm of symbolic meanings associated with these cards in divinatory readings, and look at some of their psychological connections.

4 *of* EARTHS

PART IV

Unlocking the Mysteries

12.

THE MAJOR ARCANA: UNIVERSAL SYMBOLS

Through symbolic figures and universal imagery, every Major Arcana card portrays a story or an allegory. Each reveals an important life message through interpretation or direct insight. To understand the traditional meanings of Tarot symbols and get a sense of what each card communicates, remove the Major Arcana cards from your deck and lay them all on a table. Align them face up in sequence from zero, The Fool, to twenty-one, The World. Because the Fool is numbered zero, it has the distinction of balancing alpha and omega, the first and the last, and can be placed in either the first position to be a sign of the initiation of divine play or in the last position where it reflect the assimilation of all the wisdom the Major Arcana offers.

Once you have the cards face up in front of you, it's time to make them your loyal companions for a while—or even your lifetime. As you view their images, you will become familiar with their themes, meanings, and significance. If you connect thoroughly with them, you will get to know each of them just as you would get to know a friend, and begin to see deeply into their storybook of implications. In a sense, you will learn to look at the world through their eyes and learn to hear their silent wisdom.

As you mentally dialogue with the images you will begin to unveil symbolic messages that may touch you on an emotional, mental, physical, or spiritual level. Their messages and the effect that they will have on you are unpredictable. Although there are many ways to decipher the cards' messages, popular divinatory methods include discussion of titles, symbols, colors, gender, the body language of symbolic figure(s), numbers, myths, astrological correspondences, corresponding Hebrew letters and their placement on the Tree of Life or other spiritual associations. We encourage you to form your own associations and understandings of the cards through your own life experiences.

If you seek to increase your knowledge of potential interpretations for the cards, we hope you take time to become acquainted with those we offer. For guidance in how you might discuss a card, we suggest several keywords and phrases for each one. These can serve as starting points. Ultimately, your way of relating to the cards is singularly personal and up to you.

Of the many perspectives on the cards and their meanings, some may be particularly well suited to an individual or experience, while others may apply less or not at all. You may think of other correspondences that work well. Even though this chapter is written from the perspective of a Tarot reader rather than a counselor, it blends psychological and divinatory insights. Our suggestions are only a beginning. How you use them is up to you.

Some interpretive approaches provide separate sections of meanings for cards that are drawn or placed upside down. We do not. We suggest discussing meanings of reversed cards as the direct opposite of a card's upright meanings, or use a slightly more somber tone to discuss reversed qualities. For instance, when interpreting the reversed Empress card instead of talking about her link to love in an optimistic manner, a reader may discuss the importance of finding strength when love goes askew. You may want to assess whether an upright meaning or an upside-down meaning –or for that matter, a sideways meaning— seems to fit the person who is in front of you at a given moment.

We leave it to you to discern which qualities of a card best apply to a given person or situation. If the most accurate or useful meaning is not obvious, you might mention two or three different implications of a card that might apply, and ask the person which, if any, best fits their situation.

The illustrations for the Major Arcana cards are from Anna Franklin's deck *Pagan Ways Tarot*. She has graciously allowed us to use her beautiful cards. Because her deck is based on the Celtic traditions of Britain and Ireland, some of her titles differ from the equivalent cards used in most other decks. We use the traditional names in the section headings, and then present her preferred title for the card in the text that follows.

Just the Headlines: Major Arcana Card Meanings and Connections

For each of the twenty-two cards in this chapter, we include several brief sections. *Key Ideas* offers traditional interpretations of each card in just a few lines or phrases. A paragraph of text that follows these expands those qualities into a fuller explanation of the forms in which they take shape and become visible. The *Psychological Link* to each card describes an explicit psychological perspective that can further illuminate the card's meaning and usefulness in regard to various dilemmas a person may face. Many psychological theorists and practitioners are mentioned briefly in this chapter, and if you want more information, an easy web search will bring up extensive details for all. In the last section, *Reflections*, we endeavor to connect the traditional meanings with the psychological links as we offer our own personal perspectives on the images and features of the card.[1]

0: The Fool

Key Ideas:
- Spontaneity, living in the now
- Trust in inner muses or spiritual inspiration
- Childlike innocence
- Discovering the sacred, or an inner sanctuary
- Free spiritedness, independence
- Refusal to conform

The Fool, who may be viewed as wise or foolish, understands the algorithms of sacred geometry that liberate the mind from mundane matters. Free of expectations and critical mindedness, he or she astutely observes the meandering path of life, without getting lost in hectic demands of outer situations. Embracing the moment and trusting the timeless wisdom of living in the now activates a greater understanding of how past, present, and future connect with a winning hand of cards in day-to-day existence. Standing at a distance from financial woes or emotional worries, the Fool effortlessly balances yin and yang, the negative and the positive, the feminine and masculine energies. Disengaged from society's "shoulds," the inner spirit is free to soar to unknown heights beyond the world of conventional rules and empty promises.

Psychological Link: Gestalt Therapy
(Developed by Fritz and Laura Perls)

This approach emphasizes developing immediate awareness of Gestalt therapy attends to present experience even when referring to other times and places. The "paradoxical theory of change" states that by becoming truly aware of what you are doing now, you may realize what you would rather do instead. This enables people to clarify cloudy communication within their selves, release old complexes, awaken helpful new behavior, and improve interactions with others. When a person recognizes self-defeating behavior as it is occurring, it becomes possible to substitute more sensible and effective outlooks, attitudes, and actions.

Reflections

The adventurous Fool standing by a precipice encounters many a crossroads where fate is uncertain. Listening to the heart's wisdom, he or she trusts intuition to know which path holds the most promise. Carrying only one small knapsack of alluring charm, he or she is often an eccentric who has left the baggage of hypocrisy far behind. Perhaps this is why in medieval courts, Fools, also called Jesters, were often wise men in disguise who held counsel with the king.

Another image is the Fool as the joker who makes others laugh when openly speaking about the hidden underbelly of egocentric ills. Going against taboos, he or she playfully illuminates the foolishness of those who parade blatant signs of unfettered arrogance and soul ignorance. (The Sufi Mullah Nasrudin is a celebrated example.) We see yet another aspect of this figure in Yoav Ben-Dov's remark that "The Fool can be you or me, or any other person walking the path of life. The card can be a reminder that in front of the great mysteries of existence, we are all just mindless fools."[2]

We can also connect the Fool with Alejandro Jodorowsky's statement: "Become one with the ocean of the unconscious. You will know then a state of superconsciousness in which there will be no missed action or accident. Space will no longer be a concept; you will become space. You will have no concept of time . . . there is only pure action in the eternal present."[3] At such moments, a Fool experiences the nonverbal reality of true liberation.

I. The Magician

Key Ideas:
- Power of the mind
- Quick thinking
- New beginnings or communications
- Owning your personal magic
- Creative Exploration
- Healing

The Magician, first card in the Major Arcana, is linked with taking initial steps on the journey toward self-actualization and fulfillment. It also points to fully expressing your special talents and abilities and turning dreams into realities. Also known as "The Trickster," The Magician can serve helpful or mischievous ends, so beware of falling prey to sleight-of-hand schemes that can trap you in a maze of illusion, perhaps dazzling you with one hand while the other picks your pocket or steals your heart. When facing the power of your own or others' magic, responding with kindness and compassion will help guide you to the path of integrity.

Psychological Link: Self-Actualization Theory
Abraham Maslow distinguished between survival needs and being needs. The former point to the necessary fulfillment of basic human needs, including physiological needs and safety and security, and a measure of love and belongingness. Being needs include self-esteem, and full use of talents, skills, and potentials.

Reflections
The Magician embodies our potential for self-mastery, healing, insightful communications, and soul evolution. Clever and quick minded, he or she combines the alchemical elixirs of knowledge and power in order to travel beyond the ordinary and mundane. Almost anything is possible

for the Magician, who knows how to invoke the four elements and stimulate the mind with new ideas. With Mercurial wings, such a person can carry hopes and intentions into an enchanted world of splendor. Conversely, self-deception can hinder, diminish, or block magically creative powers. For those who use their influence to serve the masters of greed, manipulation, and disregard for the higher purposes of life, a central challenge is to move from using personal power to fulfill self-centered ego demands toward developing maturity and soulful wisdom.

II. The High Priestess

Key Ideas:
- Connecting with your Higher Self
- Trusting your emotions and intuition
- Spiritual energies rising from within
- Esoteric knowledge and mysteries
- Communication with silence
- Truthfulness, purity, austerity

The High Priestess signifies spiritual mastery over material conflicts, and the wisdom of trusting your instincts and intuition. She is a symbol of uncommon passion, of finding and focusing on what is most deeply meaningful to you, and the quest to live by the guidance of inner spirit—or if you prefer, the Divine or Great Spirit. Eternally dancing in light waves of cosmic reflections, she can be perceived as the maiden or the crone, the psychologist or sorceress. She embodies feminine wisdom that can transcend the narrow confines of judgment and limitations of the logical mind.

Psychological Link: Sacred Psychology
This involves the transformation of consciousness through balancing mind and spirit, the conscious and the subconscious, and harmonizing left and right brain thinking. Jean Shinoda Bolen, Jungian Analyst, illuminates this far-reaching path in her work involving synchronicity, archetypes, and spirituality. It includes ongoing self-examination, and often, meditation and deliberation before taking action.

Reflections

Guardian of ancient rites, transitions and passages, the High Priestess stands between the material and spiritual worlds, reminding us to treasure the gifts in each moment. Sensitive, kind, and caring, she brightens the hearts of those around her with uplifting compassion, peace and joy. Veiled in mystery and secrecy, she coyly reveals her wisdom only when you are ready to respond to the nonverbal language of the heart, and can hear truth beyond the spoken word. Although she abides in the lotus of inner peace, her Artemis bow and its golden arrows are poised and ready to strike at the cruel and merciless. Her knowledge illuminates the path of balance between conscious and subconscious awareness to bring understanding of higher truth and rise above worldly confusion.

III. The Empress

("The Lady" in this deck)
Key Ideas:
- Mother figure or archetype
- Openhearted communication
- Love's potential, as seductiveness or commitment
- Creative thinking that leads to action
- Relationship guidance
- Reconciliation of opposites
- Fertility, both literally and metaphorically

The Empress, usually linked with nurturing and compassion, symbolizes forces of internal and external love that can bring self-acceptance, happiness, and personal growth. She is a sign of both literal and metaphoric fertility, and of rebirth of spring or emotional energies. In the garden of love she cultivates the ability to trust. She guides and oversees undertakings with concern for the well-being of all people and living beings, including animals, flowers, fields, and forests. The card shown here is titled "The Lady" rather than "The Empress" to suggest that it is immature to mentally raise yourself above someone else. She is an incarnation of Mother Earth, linking us together by her invisible shimmering web of Oneness.

Psychological Link: Teaching Children Emotional Intelligence in Schools

Diana Divecha, Marc A. Brackett, and their colleagues at the Yale Center for Emotional Intelligence are heart-centered educators who teach people to harness the power of emotions to create a more effective and compassionate society. In the center's "RULER" method, families, schools, and communities work together to support children's healthy emotional development to achieve their fullest potential. The approach teaches parenting skills, how to combat bullying, and studies how specific emotional intelligence skills drive attention and learning, relationship quality, and better performance.

Reflections

The Empress, who is skilled at providing what others need and want, is a symbol of universal love. Her unconditional caring for humanity has the power to heal, help, and make right what has gone wrong. When angry, she may appear to be rigid and commanding, but even then her loving heart is mostly in control. Seeing through the undulating waves in the oceanic depths of consciousness, her quest to heal the suffering of humanity usually outweighs desires for gaining external power, glory, glamorous gowns, and outrageously expensive jewelry. Alternatively, this card may stand for a grandmother or nurturing elder, with the inclusion of the whole spectrum of possible grandmotherly qualities.

The Emperor

("The Lord" in this deck)
Key Ideas:
- Control, leadership
- Influence, power, assertiveness
- Worldly success and fame
- Financial gain
- Patriarchal responsibilities
- Logic, thinking (Logos), and order

The Emperor typifies fatherly wisdom, masculine authority, earthly productivity, and worldly understanding. Accountable for the welfare of those around him, he is most effective when he cultivates open-mindedness and flexibility in himself and his communications with others. To counter inflexibility, lack of caution, and the impulse to dominate, he is counseled by those who sit at his round table to listen to the wisdom of the majority rather than riding roughshod over it or others. In the card shown here he becomes "The Lord," counterpart to The Lady, who communes in a spirit of mutuality and service that honors the indwelling spirit of humanity and nature.

Psychological Link: Freudian Psychology and the defense mechanisms
Sigmund Freud, the father of psychoanalysis, is responsible for recognizing that the mind has unconscious and conscious processes, and mechanisms to think well of yourself regardless of whether your actions are helpful or harmful to yourself or others. He put psychotherapy on the map.

Reflections
The role of Emperor may be attained by brilliance and ability, by inheritance, war or a *coup d'etat*, or by pathological scheming and dishonesty. History provides examples of all of the above. The Emperor's greatest challenge is to act for the good of all rather than out of egotism, and to demonstrate kindness rather than a sense of personal importance and self-glorification. Some, with Herculean personalities and physical strength, have an "I must be Number One" complex. But those with mature wisdom transcend the motives that drive lesser kings, and are inspired to act with deep caring and the wish to best serve their communities. The steady strength from such an Emperor brings blessings to those he encounters while traversing his own formidable path to awakening the god within. Alternatively, this card may stand for a grandfather, with the spectrum of possible grandfatherly qualities.

V. The Heirophant
("Elder" in this deck)
Key Ideas:
- Spiritual teacher or mystical leader
- Connecting with a higher purpose
- Education and gathering information
- Commitment/devotion to a religious ideology
- Spiritual-worldly integration
- Karmic or charismatic attraction

Also known as the High Priest, Pope, or Shaman, The Heirophant represents the ideal of living the truth of your higher purpose and the visible reality of spiritual laws and Higher philosophies. At best, he sees through religious differences and channels, or communicates universal truths acknowledged by all religions and great spiritual masters. By contrast, if small-minded and self-righteous, while defending religious laws and doctrines, he may blindly equate his orthodox views as "right" and everyone else as "wrong." The corresponding card shown in this deck is called "The Elder." He may embody the spirit of all religious traditions, or none, harvesting his wisdom from daily life and observation. In either case he teaches all who care to listen, and offers his wisdom to all who care to learn.

Psychological Link: Transpersonal Psychology
This involves understanding the spiritual side of existence, combining complementary aspects of science and religion. Mystical experiences, the spiritual path, and transcendent and ecstatic states of consciousness are included in its explorations.

Reflections
Striving to transcend mundane temptations, some religious leaders follow genuinely compassionate paths while others mistake religious imperialism and pious materialism for true spirituality. Parroting truths spoken by great souls, while standing on the pulpit of self-righteousness, can easily be mistaken for real concern for other people and living beings. Kindness, nonviolence, and seeking to understand one's soul essence through a meditative path help to discard such illusions. A true high

priest, often a fatherly patriarch although he can be a young person wise beyond chronological years, is a guide to finding truth beyond sectarianism. He is a supportive friend to all who seek to open the door to truth, service, and enlightenment.

VI. The Lovers

Key Ideas:
- Love, passion, intimacy
- Open-minded communications
- Choices to consider
- Important relationships
- Dependency and commitment
- Mutual respect for the other's individuality

This card's title speaks to the excitement and intricacies of Eros: seduction, love, romance, and intimate relationships. Other card meanings include becoming aware of the commitment it takes to make an important, soul-felt choice, whether to open your mind to the possibilities of love or to hide your feelings, or some other passion-filled matter. Even if the attraction of opposites makes the best path of the heart uncertain, it reminds you to enjoy life, take your time, and choose carefully. The Lovers can take consensual and mutually respectful lovemaking into a blissful realm where heartfelt caring is the norm and human love becomes divine.

Psychological Link: Humanistic Psychology

The importance of personal choice and the expansion of consciousness are central in this holistic approach to understanding the self. Each person is held responsible for his or her own choices rather than trying to pin consequences on others. You let go of desires about what and how you want another person to be, and instead discover who he or she truly is. Can your heartfelt connections offer you the sweet taste of ambrosia from the cup of unconditional love?

Reflections

Which counts most for you now, following the path of your independence or sharing intimacy and emotions with another? This card is called "choices" in some early decks. It shows the magnetism of a partner, yet invites you to ask whether or not the flame of desire can survive the warming and cooling, the attraction and repulsion, and the ups and downs of reality. Will daily life support your enchanted dreams of an ideal relationship? What must you do to live a life of passion and to feel content with the choices you've made? If you're in a relationship, what does each of you give in order to be with the other and make the relationship right for both partners? Are you just responding to the other's persona (facade, or presenting self), or do you know his or her depths? Do you accept the other "as is?" If not, what expectations, requirements, or conditions do you have for him or her—and vice versa? Choosing to be with someone you intend to "make over" to meet your criteria seldom works. Meeting another on a soulful level entwines the inner dimensions of body, mind, and emotions.

VII. The Chariot

Key Ideas:
- Travel; driving forces that propel you forward or enable you to return home after being away
- Dualistic desires or conflicting impulses
- Progress; adventure; transformational energy
- Triumph over stagnation
- An inner journey to find your center or equilibrium

The Chariot's wheels can carry you toward greater understanding of the self and fewer worries concerning unknown outcomes. After all, a "no" can become a "yes" or a "yes" can turn into a "no" in regard to either inner or outer realities. Adventurously moving toward opportunities, the charioteer steers his or her hopes along the route that seems to hold the best chance to fulfill ambitions. Pulled by opposing forces, the triumphant turning of the wheels of progress depends on the delicate balancing of opposite ideas, feelings, or desires. The horses (or sphinx) pulling the vehicle in different directions sometimes indicate a conflict between conscious intentions and unconscious instincts that lurk beneath the surface of awareness.

Psychological Link:
Eric Fromm's polarity approach
(Showing that almost every human quality can be expressed in either positive or negative ways)
Fromm's polarity approach shows that many personal qualities can be expressed in varying degrees along a continuum from very helpful to very harmful. He identified eight central needs: effectiveness; excitation and stimulation; identity; frame of orientation; relatedness with others; rootedness (feeling at home in a world from which we feel alienated); transcendence, and unity. He claims, "The mature response to the problem of existence is love."

Reflections
Your social environment contains moving forces of light and darkness that may attract you, repel you, or do both those things at once. Being steadfast in your self-determination helps you to reach your chosen destination. Be wary when others try to take control of your course of action. Your own maturity is essential in guiding the acceleration of the wheels of progressive self-evolution. Listen to the wise counsel of your intuition to avoid acting in a heedless manner. Carefully consider how you plan to reach your destination and the value of your ultimate quest as you mobilize your energy to realize your dreams. Working to respect others' needs and those of the living Earth as well as your own brings victory to all.

VIII: Strength

(Major Arcana card XI in some decks)

Key Ideas:

- Courage, mental and or physical strength
- Believing in yourself; personal empowerment
- Self-mastery; passion to create
- Generosity and charm
- Warm, extraverted energy
- The taming of unhelpful impulses

In many decks the Strength card shows a young woman and a lion standing peacefully beside each other. Here a wolf and a bear join the lion. The woman knows she cannot subdue them with physical force, but tames them with a pure and loving heart. Strength involves courage, fortitude, and mastery of inner emotions to confidently ride the waves of positive and negative, waxing and waning life forces, including acceptance of the pain as well as the pleasures of the body. Connected with solar power, the ultimate source of life, it is sometimes linked with control or domination over others. But real strength comes from power over one's self and an integration of feminine and masculine energies born from a firm yet gentle touch rather than a threat or a punch from a fist.

Psychological Link:
Martin Seligman's "Positive Psychology"
Seligman studied the strengths and virtues needed to help people experience meaningful and happy lives. Guiding a client from unhappiness to happiness is the goal. His concept of "signature strengths" involves building on what you do well. Stepping out of power struggles in order to help others feel good helps you feel good too. By contrast, glorifying yourself while putting others down deadens the love and kindness within you and stunts your ability to walk on the sunny side of life.

Reflections

Strength can mean courageously facing what you or others fear, whether the fears are about what's in front of us now, or ghosts from our past, or vague but unsettling prophecies. Some decks show a woman who stands beside a lion, or even rides it. The lion may refer to unruly others or to the fierce energy she must face to confront her own feelings of weakness in order to develop her latent potentials and possibilities. Unafraid to love a beast, she understands our interconnectedness with the forces of nature. The infinity sign above her head in many decks shows her sublime sense of values. It also shows adeptness at moving people and events away from confusions, fears, and furies into beneficial worldly and spiritual pathways. Astutely attentive to what is needed in the moment, she has the power to transform blind instincts and aggression that dwell somewhere within each of us into intelligence, intuitive wisdom, and caring.

IX. The Hermit

Key Ideas:

- Independence, freedom, humility
- Wisdom that clarifies the mysteries of life
- Pausing to reflect before forging ahead
- Letting go of the quest for status and fortune
- Ending mistaken commitments
- A search for timeless truths

The Hermit spends time cultivating a pure mind and a strong sense of responsibility and accountability. Connecting with soul wisdom, he or she searches for answers that illuminate the path to awakening higher consciousness. At home in solitude, he or she listens to the messages of elders, children, plants, animals, rivers, and mountains as a means to plumb the depths of the subconscious self and the world of spirit. Knowing how to listen in an unprejudiced way to others' views, the Hermit transcends the narrow mindedness of judgmental attitudes and accepts others for who they are. Whether a wise person, sage, or saint, the Hermit follows the inner path to find serenity and spiritual benefit.

Psychological Links: Existential philosophy
(As presented by Soren Kierkegaard, Jean-Paul Sartre, and Simone de Beauvoir)
Existentialism includes freedom of the self; thinking for your self about traditions; taking personal responsibility and making decisions based on inner, authentic being. The Hermit is often equated with the Greek philosopher *Diogenes the Cynic*, who distrusted society's truisms, greed, and hypocrisy. His lamp is said by some to reflect a search for truth, and by others a search for an honest human being.

Reflections
The Hermit may refer to habits of asceticism, renunciation, and detachment from everyday desires and cravings. He or she follows a quest for spirit rather than for material riches. Seeing the God-self in others, and in the glistening cosmic web that connects the souls of all, he or she has found, or is searching for, eternal values that transcend cultures and societies.

Or on a more practical level, this image may indicate that you are standing alone or are having a hard time making contact with others. Linked with the ability to draw on inner resources, it also points to gaining greater self-acceptance and focusing on your inner being. Feeling grateful for what you have, instead of resentment for what you don't, can light the lamp of happiness. Meditation is the Hermit's tool of choice for reflection, improving perspectives, developing mind control, and finding serenity.

X. The Wheel of Fortune

("Wyrd" in this deck)
Key Ideas:
- Good fortune; good luck
- Evolving circumstances
- Heightened awareness or a new potential
- Opportunity for success
- A turning point
- Coming face to face with the unknown

Three goddesses, called Wyrd, weave the ever-changing web of personal destiny. Associated with the ever-spinning wheel of life and the evolving and revolving circle of fortune, this card can indicate change, chance, and new possibilities. Whether downward energy moves upward and you feel on top of the world or upward energy begins to descend and you feel at your lowest, the inscription on the ring the Sufi Attar gave to a powerful king holds true: "This too shall pass."[4]

Because the center of the rotating wheel is associated with the all-seeing eye of Cosmic Creation, it is linked with personal growth, greater knowledge, and expansion of awareness. We can find peace by focusing on the still center of the wheel, or we can bind ourselves to experiencing the highs and lows of its outside edge as it carries us round and round, forward to our uncertain destiny.

Psychological Link: Kurt Lewin's *Field Theory*
(That identifies the physical and psychological force-fields within which we live)

Lewin identified forward and restraining movements of the forces of life that can impede or help you, slow your movement or aid your progress. He named choices between two attractive options approach-approach conflicts, between two unattractive ones avoidance-avoidance conflicts, and situations that carry both a promise of rewards and the likelihood of pain approach-avoidance conflicts.

Reflections

The Wheel is connected to another metaphor: the end of one chapter of a story and the beginning of another; or on a smaller scale, turning to the next page.

Because it gathers momentum in the direction of progress we can usually be optimistic about what we might find as we make our way toward the future—but also it is wise to be alert to possible missteps. Even when the spinning Wheel of Fortune stands still, we wonder about what opportunities, obstacles, or adventurous situations we may face. What can we do to bring about the results we seek? But at times, as the wheel turns, we must let go of our attachments to hoped for results and accept what life brings. Even if destiny is uncertain or not playing out as you would like, when the hand of Fate offers a favorable moment, sometimes you can seize it like an acrobat grasps a passing brass ring as it swings through the air, and enjoy your good luck. After all, the sound the wheel makes as it turns is the ancient message *Carpe Diem*: "seize the day."

XI. Justice

(Major Arcana card VIII in some decks)
Key Ideas:
- Agreement between one's inner and outer self
- Weighing pros and cons; mediation
- Attaining a just and fair resolution
- Integrity, honesty, and trust
- Harmony between feminine and masculine forces

Often Justice is depicted as a blindfolded woman holding a double-edged sword to cut through untruth in one hand, and the scales of balance to weigh the merits of actions, reactions, or non-actions on your soul-journey in the other hand. Linked with the healing power of compassionate, loving words and actions, this card is a symbolic gauge for fine-tuning inner balance, emotional values, and outer relationships. When the head and heart both draw inspiration from a higher source, clear awareness of what truly matters rises to the surface of consciousness. Being just need not necessarily mean to laud or condemn, but it can be a gauge of right and wrong and serve as a soulful guide.

Psychological Link: Alfred Adler's "Individual Psychology"
A weak, sickly child, Adler overcame early childhood handicaps to become outdoing and social. He coined the phrase, "inferiority complex," and said that few of us realize our potential because almost everyone is trying to triumph over something that is keeping them from becoming their most capable selves. Children who are neglected, abused, or spoiled face greater handicaps than others who are not. Adler viewed "social interest"—that is, acting beneficially in ways that help others—as the most valuable guiding motive in life.

Reflections

If your honesty with yourself has been asleep, the perceptive blade of wisdom that cuts through self-deception to liberate truth can awaken it. Weighing the merits of alternatives, the pros and the cons, can help improve and fine tune decision-making. But the reasonable voice of Justice advises peace above conflict and tells you that everything you want to possess is just smoke in the wind compared to who you are and are becoming. The Sufi mystic Attar said, "You truly possess only what will not be lost in a shipwreck." With perseverance, your energies subtle and strong, earthly and divine, and the spiritual and physical can merge to become integrated in a balanced state of mind that allows you to accept your true self for who you are.

XII. The Hanged Man

Key Ideas:
- Being hung-up in some way
- Suspending action; meditating on your directions
- Being tested; endurance; sacrifice
- Selfless, sacred, or austere actions
- Surrendering to what is; letting go
- A familiar perspective turned upside-down

Finding something of benefit, or success in a relationship can result from seeing and sensing your situation from a viewpoint different from the norm. You may feel the need to reverse your course of action, or feel suspended between one physical or psychological "place" and another. You might sacrifice or surrender something you value for an ethical or social cause in order to obtain something of greater consequence. Choosing to question or abandon old patterns of thought, action, or self-imposed boundaries can ignite new possibilities.

Psychological Link: C.G. Jung
(who founded Analytical Psychology)
Jung focused on the sacredness of the psyche. Among many other concepts, he developed the theories of archetypes, the collective

unconscious, synchronicity, individuation, and the inner balancing of positive and negative forces. He found that developing your underdeveloped sides is an important key to creativity. The Hanged Man card may also represent Jung's "wounded healer" archetype, or point to an unresolved, entrenched complex that the time has come to heal or discard.

Reflections

Many of us live our days and nights in clichés and conformity, limited by narrow views of our potentials. Consumed with mundane routines we forget to explore our depths where we can connect with healing currents of universal energy. The Hanged Man steps out of the daily humdrum to develop "mindfulness" or "witness consciousness" and watch the mind and emotions in action. Giving yourself permission to leave behind what is no longer serving your best interest may open previously unseen dimensions of your self, your life, and/or your relationships. Yet in so doing, listen to the voice of your own intuition, especially when you are (or someone else is) asking for some sacrifice that leaves your soul naked in the snow and doesn't feel right.

XIII: Death

Key Ideas:
- Transformation, purging decay
- Intense or exciting change
- Death; rebirth; regeneration
- Endings; bereavement
- Reflection on what truly matters
- Sunset of opportunity, setting a new course

When viewing the Death card, many people tremble in fear of the potential loss of friends, family, lovers, or even their own self. To focus on "fear factors" brings anxiety. Instead, you can use this card to explore healing a person's death related fears, wounds or anxieties, or work through the pain of a real loss. Also, if appropriate, you can talk about this card in relation to its symbolic connection to transformation, rebirth, unexpected change, or letting go of the past memories that are blocking enjoyment of the present. Often people smile when you guide the discussion to potential for future opportunities, renewal, and fulfilling transformations, like a phoenix that rises from the ashes.

Psychological link: Elizabeth Kubler-Ross
(Authority on Death and Survivors)
The Swiss-born American psychiatrist who wrote the book *On Death and Dying* outlined her research on the five stages of grief that are typically experienced by dying patients. Her later research extended her work on death to include any major transition where some type of loss was experienced. She advises that when someone you love (or even a dear pet) dies, mourn fully. Then at your own pace, let yourself reopen to live a full life again, keeping your best memories of the one who passed as a lasting gift to illuminate your own life.

Reflections.
The Grim Reaper's scythe sweeps away dying vines and dead leaves of years gone by to let fresh green shoots on the Tree of Life reach toward the sun. An old saying goes, "Those most afraid of death are those who have not lived fully." There is at least a grain of truth in that. Are you deadening your aliveness by not doing something that you would find exciting, fulfilling, and desirable? Are all too familiar inner voices or outside people telling you *"Don't do that!"* even though it would harm no one? Invoke renewal and positive transformation by letting the dread of death, inevitable change, or/and decaying situations fall from the vision of how you see your world. After all, Death can be viewed as the Great Renewer who frees the spirit to rekindle the flames of soul knowledge.

XIV: Temperance

Key Ideas:
- Finding the center between contact and avoidance
- Cooperation in relationships
- Reconciliation of opposites and disagreements
- Moderation: Enough and not too much
- Living in harmony with nature
- Balancing untamed impulses

The winged angel on the white horse in this picture refers to having been through a difficult period and entering a time of healing, forgiveness, and blessing. It differs from many decks, which show a woman standing with one foot on land and another in a pool or stream of water. Wise beyond logic, Temperance personifies the fearless power to step into the depths of the subconscious (the pool of reflecting water) while keeping her balance standing in a fertile field (the conscious mind). Combining the qualities of love, discipline, and moderation to perfect the soul's journey, this guardian of the heart's wisdom displays the freedom to live and express truth outside the realm of conventional concepts of time and space.

Psychological Link: Psychology of the Body

Wilhelm Reich, Stanley Keleman, and Eleanor Criswell all showed in different ways that our mind, emotions, and body are intimately connected. Reich, who coined the term muscular armor found that we lock our emotional responses into our muscular tension and relaxation. Keleman advanced Reich's work and brought it to a broad audience. Criswell, known for pioneering work in Somatic Psychology and Somatic Yoga, has worked to highlight balancing the mind and the body to actively control physiological processes. Somatic awareness enables people to become more effective in daily affairs, and healing body, personal and interpersonal problems, and in the tempering of desires and aversions.

Reflections

Temperance stands perfectly poised and balanced between sensory discipline and the transpersonal self who lives beyond the cravings and illusions of the ego. Although she is of the world, she is beyond its dualities, its limitations, and tethers. Equated with balanced spiritual and material forces, she listens before speaking, and accepts the unraveling of fate, neither imposing her truth on others nor letting others impose theirs on her. Buddha expressed her essence as "The Middle Way" between extremes that grows out of an experience of those extremes. On the path toward finding inner truth, the virtue of self-control leads to moving through confusion and finding a synergy and natural integration among the various sides of the self.

XV: The Devil

("The Underworld" in this deck)
Key Ideas:
- Negative thinking or worries
- Temptation, greed, indulgence
- Bondage; the need to reverse circumstances
- Blame, or harmful speech
- Unacceptable impulses or actions
- Shady transactions
- Identifying with matter to the neglect of spirit

Sometimes linked with Lucifer the Antichrist, or evil, and other times with Pan, the joyful Greek horned god of natural passion and sexual pleasures, this card conveys a message of potent forces, intense behavior, or lessons to be learned. Often the Devil serves as an external projection screen for unaccepted personal anger, the dropping of an emotional bomb, potential or actual violence, or other hostile tendencies. He provides a pretext for self-righteously claiming that the Other Person is doing the Devil's work while we ourselves, are far more virtuous. The picture here is labeled "The Underworld" rather than "The Devil." This card is a positive reminder that arrogant, ignorant, or socially unacceptable impulses can be redirected toward helpful ends, or channeled to foster remarkable creativity. Coming to know our "shadow," the sides of ourselves we usually choose not to notice, is a major step on this path.

Psychological Link: Philip Zimbardo

(Who showed how powerful our immediate environment's control of our behavior can be)

Zimbardo's Stanford prison experiment included research on moral and ethical values. It demonstrated how strongly our environment and the people in it can affect our thoughts, emotions, and actions. His work includes penetrating examinations of the interpersonal, environmental, and psychological dimensions of human torture. Reflecting on his work, Zimbardo declares that the mind has "an infinite capacity to make any of us villains or heroes by enabling us to be caring or indifferent, selfless or selfish, creative or destructive."[5]

Reflections

A fallen angel kicked out of heaven, the demonic king is alleged to make us think that insincere or harmful behavior is virtuous as we become unhappy victims of our unrecognized impulses toward destructive attitudes or actions. Spiritual teachings maintain that as we acknowledge and work through our negative impulses, the Devil disappears. But for those with misguided cravings who claim to be possessed by Satan or evil spirits, it is hard for others to understand why they can't or don't want to change. Difficult as such a reality may be for the innocent to comprehend, grabbing the devil by the horns and taking this beast from the shadows into the light is the historic formula to take away its power to harm others.

XVI: The Tower

Key Ideas:
- Sudden impact of unexpected fate or karma
- Omen of impending trouble, rupture, or separation
- Ego trauma, disempowerment
- Emotional upheaval; challenge
- The death of oppressive old institutions and patterns
- A time for rebuilding

A lightning bolt strikes the tower to cause its looming structure to crumble and fall. Uncontrollable circumstances, challenges, and disappointments strike at human vulnerability. The tower points to finite, man-made constructions of life, power structures, or belief systems that won't survive over time or have outlived their usefulness. A flash of lightning displays the power of Mother Nature to illuminate a path of immediate change. Mental flexibility, and changing your outlook and actions, perhaps even radically, can turn apparent disasters into constructive paths filled with better opportunities.

Psychological Link: Aaron Beck's Cognitive Behavioral Therapy

Beck developed a psychotherapy based on observing and affecting thinking patterns. He discovered that while his patients talked to him, many also carried on an inward silent conversation with themselves that sabotaged the therapy. (For instance, "The doctor probably thinks I'm a real jerk. This work won't come to anything.") Turning those silent conversations into open discussions proved to be a key intervention to reconstruct self-defeating dialogue into more constructive and useful inner statements.

Reflections

Occasionally a thunderbolt of transformation, often driven by circumstance, strikes without warning. What was imprisoned beneath the personality's facade is released. Secrets of both the self and or the social structure of society may be revealed. Creative energies explode. Liberation, purification, and rebirth can result. Or we can hunker down and fearfully cling to old patterns that lock us into pain and suffering. When the tower starts to crumble, it can also seem a miraculous sign of divine intervention, a message to abandon preset agendas, change our present focus, and rebuild our life, or collectively, even our culture, in a manner in which mental and emotional currents are harmoniously integrated.

XVII: The Star

Key Ideas:
- Hope and optimism
- Rejuvenating your focus
- An enlightening oracle
- Awakening to truth, insight, guidance
- Clarifying perspectives or goals
- Confidence and empowerment
- Pursuit of happiness

A bright light of renewing insight emerges from deep within to increase your momentum toward the fulfillment of desires. Looking at your surroundings with gratitude ignites a radiant glow of hope to brighten your pathway and illuminate to many ideas and possibilities for deciding your best course of action. The Star also points to clarifying channels of communication with others to inspire finding answers, positive directions, and creative solutions. When questioning romance, lighten-up concerns by taking more time for fun and laughter. Learning about Tantra illuminates the unity between divine and erotic love. In the card shown here, a woman standing in a natural pool is filling a pitcher from a waterfall cascading toward her, portraying an intimate contact with care for the natural world.

Psychological Link: Virginia Satir
(The mother of family therapy)
Known for family reconstructive therapy, Satir identified counterproductive interaction patterns: blaming others, distracting attention from harmful behavior or positive possibilities, placating others at the cost of sacrificing one's own needs, and computing—that is, trying to solve everything logically while ignoring feelings. Also, she described "leveling" as a way to move from closed (typically destructive) to open (typically constructive) communication. She placed major emphasis on support for each person's self-esteem, acceptance, and appreciation of positive qualities.

Reflections
Standing in the pool of life-sustaining waters, the star struck maiden shows affinity with both this world of matter and the universal Spirit of the collective unconscious. An intimate part of infinite nature of cosmic space, she is associated with the incarnation of Nuit, the Egyptian Star Goddess who eternally watches over her counterpart, the Earth. With her longing to share the rapture of the heavens, she sets fire to heart-felt emotions to inspire us to expand our understanding of changeable currents of desire and the steadfast nature of love. Through our undertakings to find emotional happiness, we become more alert to the importance of sharing, generosity, and kindness. Clear, passionate communication unveils such opportunities, especially if we align with the starry light of awakening and our intentions are pure.

XVIII: The Moon
Key Ideas:
- Intuition and imagination
- The feminine nature and mystique
- Strong tides of emotion
- Dreams, memories, visions
- The subconscious
- Changing cycles
- Sensitivity to spiritual truths

Discovering what is submerged beneath watery realms of emotion brings a vital, intuitive, or soulful understanding of one's inner dynamics in connection with others. Deeply receptive and rich beyond imagining, the Moon illuminates a communion between the Sun and Earth, between spirit and matter. The moon is linked with the goddess Artemis, Greek goddess of the hunt. Historically the moon has been revered as sacred natural force power that can empower and protect the feminine spirit, the Mother, the maternal nature, childbirth, and the sincere of heart. Lunar energy influences our instinct to fathom subconscious depths and can strengthen or weaken our passion for either solitude or intimate communication. On the other hand, it can intensify emotional swings, and the need to balance biological rhythms. If we are too lunar, we may become "loony" and lose the ability to clearly say "no" when appropriate.

Psychological Link: Karen Horney
(Founder of Feminine Psychology)
Horney was the first to apply psychoanalysis to examine women's issues. She watched for chronic tendencies to move toward, against, or away from others as strategies to find safety. In her view we are naturally healthy and growth seeking. She held that internal problems usually begin with interpersonal problems, such as children who are manipulative, or parents who offer no guidance, are harshly critical, who break promises, and either put the child on a pedestal or fail to pay attention and recognize when the child does something good.

Reflections
Finding friends or "allies" with whom you can share your feelings can help you be attentive to focusing on your confidence instead of insecurities,

your hopes instead of fears. Developing faith in your "third eye'" enables you to find your true passion and see through illusions, discerning what's real or unreal in your dreams for tomorrow. If you find yourself going up and down about who, what, and where you are in life or in relationships, dive inward and explore your depths to find new answers to how you can best navigate the ever-changing waves in the river of life. Direct awareness of the statements and images you're creating in your mind can be helpful in countering emotional swings and in centering yourself in a balanced state of mind. Plant seeds of desires during the waning moon, weed your intentions during the waxing moon, and celebrate your growth on the full moon.

XIX: The Sun

Key Ideas:
- Positive energy; self-esteem
- Conscious awareness, leadership
- Effective action, growth
- Friendship, affection
- Enjoyment; happiness
- Inner warmth; healing
- Embracing transparency

Vitality and creative self-expression grow into blossoms of opportunity that encourage personal evolution. The Sun illuminates that which has been lost behind shadows of forgetfulness or neglect and shines brightly on the path to healing. Truths are realized that enable you to discover a dawning light of awareness. Sprouting new life, renewal, regeneration, an improved sense of self, and the connecting of kindred spirits are qualities linked to Sun energy. By discovering dormant capacities, you have more energy available to benefit both yourself and others. The Sun can inspire you to lighten-up, to remain in touch with your inner child as guide to playfulness and recreation. But there is also the danger of refusing to grow up and saying "no" to working through problems or learning from past mistakes. Even though this card can point to the possibility of mature perspectives and responsibilities, sometimes it just feels good not to worry about grown-up stuff and to do nothing but sit in the Sun's radiant splendor.

Psychological Link: Carl Rogers
"person-centered" therapy and education

"The facts are always friendly," declared one of the twentieth century's most influential psychologists. Rogers used *phenomenology* (hearing another person's experience as it is for that person) in his person-centered psychology. This approach is focused on personal growth, empowerment, and respect for others' subjective reality through "unconditional positive regard." He avoided arguments and emphasized harmony between one's surface self and deeper thoughts and feelings. "Transparency" involves expressing thoughts and feelings as one's own, not trying to disguise them as facts about another. His sunny outlook and skillful listening never made others feel "less than," but helped them find their own "sunny side."

Reflections

The Sun card is a good omen for the expansion of inner light and the successful outcome of creative efforts. When you feel down or depressed, imagine taking this image into your own heart, and allowing it to send positive energy throughout and around you. Connected with a joy that transcends unnecessary doubts, the sun's warmth removes discomforting chills. An assertive force by nature, its energy is usually expressed with a steady radiance that shines equally on the rich and the poor, the tall and the small. The risk symbolized by this card is the possibility of an attitude of being "above," or "better than" others. The sun is most beneficial when its warmth is shared gently. Because all planets in our solar system revolve around the Sun, it is perfectly centered in divine order.

XX: Judgment

("Rebirth" in this deck)
Key Ideas:
- Karma: Facing results of past actions
- Discernment
- Judgmental criticism of self or others
- Choices involving being just and fair-minded
- Learning to let go or a transitional opportunity
- Resurrection; rebirth; a new era
- Rite of passage

A powerful event(s) tests the truth of your decisions and present visions of where you see your life going. New perspectives can arise on the horizon as you appraise your current situation and time shrinks to hold you captive to past choices made with or without wise counsel. Judgments of your own or other's realities can be true, false, or somewhere in between. Being kind-minded as you make appraisals regarding the truth of your own or others' opinions helps you avoid becoming the victim of frail assumptions. Appreciating instead of condemning can herald the end of the up and down merry-go-round of illusions.

Psychological Link: Harold H. Kelley's studies of interdependence and attribution

Kelley identified rewarding and punishing patterns in relationships, and described the details of how we form impressions of others. He gave students an advance written description of a forthcoming guest speaker in which just one word was different for half the students. Some descriptions described the speaker as a rather "warm" person, while the other version described him as a rather "cold" person. Then all listened to the same talk by the same person at the same time in the same room. Those who were told he was "warm" gave his speech a significantly higher rating than those told he was "cold." Just one word changed their perception! Now consider what incessant exposure to television, other media, and group social pressures can do.

Reflections

Judgment may foreshadow a fair or unfair verdict, intervention, or decision. Advancing forward on the game board of life, there's no justification for illogic when walking the tightrope that balances the good and the bad, likes and dislikes, desire and repulsion, forgiveness and blame. An honest judge avoids all conflicts of interest and attends carefully to specifics and details rather than generalities. Who or what will be helped or harmed by one verdict or another? A judgment can be stern, merciful, and educational all at once. If your soul has been sleeping, wise judgment may awaken it.

XXI: The World

("The Universe" in this deck)

Key Ideas:

- Embracing wholeness
- Resolving past issues or conflicts
- Completion of a journey or undertaking
- New beginnings, fulfillment
- Dancing energy, deserved merit
- The vastness of consciousness
- A journey into unknown realms of possibility

In our era of space telescopes and seeing distant galaxies, this deck titles the traditional World card "The Universe." Personal empowerment strengthens selfless understanding and speeds solutions of challenging issues. Integrating pro and con realities creates an expansive outlook. Things we never dreamed of become possible as we free ourselves from self-imposed limits to perceive the possibilities of the wider world. By not locking yourself into outdated ideas or ideologies, you move forward with a greater inward sense of wholeness and outward sense of wisdom. Openness to others helps transform your perspective as you begin to see yourself not just as a separate individual but as part of a universal flow of conscious awakening.

Psychological Link: Edward Chace Tolman's concept of "cognitive maps"

Intentions and purposes were Tolman's key interests, even when studying rats in mazes. He showed how most of us form mental maps of thinking and action that box ourselves into what we already know, feel, and do, and how little we explore new paths and possibilities. Recent research proves that new neurons in the brain can grow at any age. We can open ourselves to new adventures, explore new realities, and have peak experiences in which we perceive reality as integrated and whole. Despite all evils, our magnificent world is for the most part profoundly beautiful and good.

Reflections

Consider expressing some aspect of yourself that you have considered defective or inadequate, and for this moment view it as perfect. With most human qualities there is usually a possibility of conscious growth and change in a minute, a day, or a year, but here and now you can only be as you are (although you have choices regarding specific words and actions). What mental maps have you been using to structure your personal world? Might there be any value in consciously taking different routes and replacing easy habits with more adventurous ones, with listening to the intuitive mind instead of logical perceptions? You can consciously choose to let the paths to realizing your dreams be more expansive than they have ever been. If in conflict, look for multiple perspectives that inspire heart-centered composure. Whether you travel through the world or through your inner self, look to a horizon where the sun is rising on increased prospects for your happiness.

Now we wend our way through some unexpected turns on our royal road as we move on to the imagery and incidents of the Minor Arcana.

13.

THE FOUR SUITS OF THE MINOR ARCANA: A REFLECTING POOL OF AWARENESS

When you first look at your cards, the part of the Tarot called the Minor Arcana, pip cards, or lesser mysteries resembles a deck of normal playing cards. At first glance the differences seem small. There are wands instead of clubs, cups instead of hearts, swords instead of spades, and pentacles instead of diamonds. Each suit has ten cards numbered from one to ten. And just as each suit in a playing card deck has face or court cards—a jack, a queen, and a king, each suit in a Tarot deck has a page, a knight, a king, and a queen. Although there is no division into "black" and "red" cards, the structure seems similar. And it is.

And it isn't. Whereas a six is a six with playing cards, with the Tarot a six is filled with layers of meaning. It is also embedded in a network of relationships with other cards such that in a divinatory reading its significance may affect the meaning of other cards near it in a spread. In short, each card has a distinct and sometimes complex set of connotations that offer insight into varied influences that may affect a person. Some minor cards may appear unique in relation to the artistic style of a given deck, but more often their symbolism points to universal messages that have been uttered since before calendar time.

The Wands, Swords, Pentacles, and Cups are the symbolic foundation for interpreting the Minor Arcana. Each of these four suits corresponds to a different element. The Wands correspond with fire. Swords are linked with the element air. Pentacles are earth, and Cups pour forth the element water.

As you thumb through the cards of each suit, you might want to reflect on which one is most like your own way of being in the world, as well as pondering what each suggests about your present situation or life direction. Or perhaps one suit may remind you to develop sides of yourself to which you give less thought and energy, or to take more time to explore and express your emotions or your creativity.

Here's a chart with an overview. Then we'll look at the suits one by one.

Minor Arcana Correspondence Chart

SUIT	ELEMENT	ZODIAC LINK	KEY PHRASE	PRIMARY ASSOCIATIONS
SWORDS (or Crystals)	Air-mind	Gemini Libra Aquarius	I understand	Ideas, analysis, perceptions, beliefs
WANDS (or Rods, Staves)	Fire-spirit	Aries Leo Sagittarius	I create	Action, will-power, fiery energy, passion
CUPS (or Chalices)	Water-emotions	Cancer Scorpio Pisces	I love	Emotions, intuition, imagination, receptivity
PENTACLES (or Discs, Coins)	Earth-body	Taurus Virgo Capricorn	I make	Work, finances, prosperity, environment

PAGE of SWORDS

The Cutting Edge: The Suit of Swords

A sword is a symbol for the element Air, which is linked to the strength of ideas and the airy astrological Sun signs of Gemini, Libra, and Aquarius. In the Minor Arcana, this suit, sometimes viewed as "the swords of reason," traditionally represents the world of thought. One side of its double-edged blade refers to analysis and reason used to solve problems and decide on actions. Its piercing force can be like the moment when dawn's first light dissolves night's darkness as our thinking mind penetrates to the core of a matter. But with the other side of the blade we can get lost in worries about the future, regrets about the past, confusion about present choices, and other mental tangles.

Those two sides of the sword, however, leave out its third dimension, which is crucial. At the blade's tip is a sharp point. It reflects another aspect of mind, our capacity to slice through the veils, mists and clouds of mistaken concepts that can cause great upset, both for us and for others. The sword's point reminds us to use our faculty of direct awareness to see and hear what is actually happening in and around us. As we do, we breathe freely, rather than suffocating in our worries. When we are mindful in the present moment, we perceive reality directly. We are united with our mind in action.

The suit of Swords also holds clues about how we think and what we communicate. What kind of energy do we share? Are we determined to win at any cost, to dominate others even if it requires intentional harshness and cruelty? Or, are we respectful, considerate, and even joyful?

With every card in the suit of swords, there are many possibilities for better understanding. These include cutting through to the essence of a situation to find an answer, a creative solution, or a creative image. There might be a warning about challenges or difficulties that can trigger useful critical analysis rather than letting us stagnate in a mental haze, or sever false thinking with direct awareness and understanding of what's going on in a situation.

KNIGHT of WANDS

Playing with Fire: The Suit of Wands

Fiery energy is the essence of this suit, also called rods, staves, batons, or fire in different decks. Connected with the element fire and the zodiac signs of Aries, Leo, and Sagittarius, it represents willpower, determination, perseverance, and creativity. "Get things moving" or "Let's keep moving" are this suit's watchwords. They can be a wake-up call to rouse yourself out of lethargy and start putting energy into actions that will bring about the ends you hope to realize.

Or when you're discouraged, and afraid that you'll never achieve your dreams, it can be like the directive in the *I. Ching,* "perseverance furthers." In other words, don't give up. Major results seldom come from minor effort.

Sometimes the appearance of the suit of Wands is a sign that your energy is rising like smoke or you're "smokin' hot." Or you may need to engage your passion, or cook up some sizzling, creative ideas. Perhaps brainstorming new insights will help you rethink what you're trying to do, or take your plans to a higher level. You may need to consider different perspectives or methods, or go more deeply into those you've already established. To connect more with your energies, you might sit in meditation next to a sacred fire—or at least a candle flame. A unique vision might just jump from its flames. And because this suit is linked with the heart's desire to shine like a star, you may go beyond what you know is possible into the realm of unsuspected possibilities.

Amid your drive, passions, fickle flirtations, ambitions, and victories, be aware that as you strive to achieve your goals, those who help others also help themselves. Holding a hand of cards with many wands invokes the eternal flame of spirit and the universal oneness of humanity.

But when fiery forces become too intense, the suit of wands can point to problems involving competitiveness, aggression, or anger. These cards can signal a tendency to become heated too fast, or aggressive too easily, whether with words or actions. At such times, remember the principle of "mirror neurons." That is, the emotional tone you direct toward others is likely to trigger the same emotional tone in them toward you. When fiery energy is too hot, you can remind yourself to make a cooling commitment to enjoy your gift of life as it is. After all, a flame doesn't have to be on "high" to scramble an egg. If you're fueled by the energy of the suit of wands, from time to time you probably need to remind yourself to pause, breathe deeply, and take it easy for a while. Then you can speak or act from a rational or even caring or loving place instead of getting over-heated and worked up about everything. When you're not only passionate and animated, but also sensitive to what's going on in the people and places around you, you're likely to find yourself more often lighting the torch of victory.

QUEEN of CUPS

Delights and Challenges of Love: The Suit of Cups

At times called Chalices, Goblets, or the suit of the heart, Cups are associated with emotions, romance, intimacy, affection, seduction, and most especially love, the great elixir of life. Although it's nice to think of this suit as equal to new love, enduring commitments, and delicious moments, it doesn't ignore heartbreaking romances or difficult relations. Besides love, the Cups are discussed in relation to empathy, intuition, unseen currents of feelings that emerge from the caverns of our psyches, and the zodiac water signs of Cancer, and Scorpio, and Pisces.

The use of the title "Chalices" for this suit in some decks is intriguing. The most celebrated chalice of all is the Holy Grail, said by some to be the vessel from which Jesus drank at the Last Supper. As such, it embodies the transcendent, healing light of compassion. It's shimmering illumination floats in surging waves reflected in the qualities of kindness, humility, and caring for others that have been and are regarded by many spiritual masters and saints as the very essence of enlightenment.

Receiving or not receiving unconditional love and caring is one of the first events in every infant's life. The kind and quality of love and other emotions experienced during childhood, especially from parents or other caretakers, often places an enduring stamp on a person's character. What is learned in those early years can affect the way a person reacts to others throughout life. In some way, every day feeling or not feeling loved reaches deep into the core of the soul. This is why insight into matters of the heart is so vital to card interpretation.

But even if we tend to deify love, we can't just turn on the tap and demand that the cup fill our expectations. To become truly loving there are emotional lessons we need to learn and watery forces we must endure. Difficult romantic issues, betrayal, and loss can intensify currents of emotional flow. Overly dependent love or insecure, demanding, possessive, or domineering love can pose diverse challenges. Softening those patterns and moving toward love that truly respects others' wants and needs as well as your own love generates fewer complications and is a real blessing.

When others sense conscious open-hearted love, they tend to be magnetically attracted to it. "Love thy neighbor as thyself," advised Jesus. Such love can also be called *unconditional love, for nothing need be done to earn it.* For the most part, the quest to develop such understanding and to be able to interpret the sometimes veiled, unspoken messages of the heart is a path toward insight into the meanings of the Cups and their emotional issues.

"Will I find love?" and "What will happen in my relationship?" are among the most frequent questions that any reader will hear. Similarly, "Why am I having trouble finding a good relationship?" or "Why are my partner and I having so many problems?" are questions central to both the Tarot and counseling sessions. Without doubt many of the curves, peaks, and valleys of love will need to be addressed when discussing the flowing nature of emotions. We often tell Tarot students that when you can wisely discuss this suit of the heart, you are ready to offer readings to others.

The suit of Cups can also indicate delving into the world of dreams, the subterranean realms of our unconscious minds, and understanding, developing, and using our intuitive abilities. Although they are latent in everyone, many of us learned as children to suppress our intuitive abilities because often they led us to speak inconvenient truths at inopportune times. For many, the cups can point to the importance of recovering them, often making it easier to be perceptive of the heart's truths.

KING of DISKS

Making a Living and Living on Earth: The Suit of Pentacles

Called Disks, Coins, or Pentacles, this suit is linked with the element earth and the zodiac Sun signs Capricorn, Taurus, and Virgo. One Spanish-language deck calls the suit "Oros," or "Golds." But labeling this suit in reference to money artificially narrows its meaning, as traditionally it is also linked with common sense, practicality, responsibility, security, safety, physical efforts, tangible gains, property, the material world, protection, and Mother Nature herself.

Certainly, however, money matters to most of us and many do indeed have questions and worries about financial affairs and material prosperity. Whatever you call this suit, key concerns are helping people look deeply into issues involving their jobs, promotions, whether to change careers, how to handle a business situation or whether to stay in their present home or move to a new one—or even a different city.

Besides worldly realities, this suit can refer to concerns regarding the body, be they large or small, and about how life affects you on physical levels. Common are questions about illness, injury, and longevity. Inquiries involving health problems require special care. Legally, answers to such questions may not include medical suggestions or ideas that are likely to bring physical results, but you can refer the person to a specialist or healer in the area of concern. If the cards and the person's response suggest an unwanted yet inevitable outcome, your work may center on offering tools or perspectives that can help work through fears and difficult feelings.

Another dimension of pentacles is the earth itself. You may be an avid outdoors person or someone who lives confined within the walls of an office who has lost much of your connection with nature. Either way this suit can remind you to go where you can sense the earth beneath your feet. For example, the Ace of Pentacles might point toward taking a trip to the countryside, starting a food or flower garden in the backyard, placing planting boxes on an apartment windowsill, or even climbing a mountain. When you feel the tree and plant spirit of life all around you, you're more likely to be in touch with your own rootedness and connection with the harmonious rhythms of nature.

This suit can also refer to the qualities of being grounded, patient, and rooted like a tree to your own sense of balance and creativity. An earthly foundation enables you to feel sure and steady inwardly and/or to develop fine craftsmanship—or give care and attention to each detailed step of a concrete project.

Pentacles also remind us to carefully notice our own sensations and actions in here-and-now physical reality and not to get lost in a myriad of fantasies of other possibilities. What is real in this place and this moment? What do you truly need to exist and how do you structure your world to provide it? Just scratching the soil with a rake seldom turns up gold. What can you do to find or create practical solutions that can improve some part of your tangible reality, or make a difference for others or your ecosystem?

A grasp of both the obvious dimensions and subtle details of each suit offers a good start toward understanding the minor cards. The next step is to learn more about the numbered cards in each of the four suits. From one to ten, each number has certain qualities attributed to it. Put a suit and a number together and suddenly you enter a new reality—a world where numbers themselves have meanings and implications. There are also coherent themes that tie the numbers of the four suits together, and you're about to find out what those are.

14.

IF NUMBERS COULD SPEAK, WHAT MIGHT THEY SAY?

What's in a number? Not much, you might think. Or, a mathematician such as Pythagoras might reply, mysterious and marvelously meaningful worlds within worlds. Yet again, a stockbroker will offer a completely different answer.

There are diverse systems of numerology that assign meanings and qualities to each number. Some are similar and some are not. For instance, some attributes suggested for a specific number in Vedic numerology are quite different than those given to the same number in Chinese numerology. In China, the number eight is considered a lucky number, but in Vedic numerology eight is the number of lessons to be learned. And that's just a beginning of a long discussion, as there are various ancient traditions that have beliefs about what secrets the numbers hold. But we won't go into all that here.

In the mystical world of the Tarot, we find that there is a history of generally accepted meanings for the numbers on its cards. Learning some of these associations gives insight into how we might interpret a card and understand its relationship to others.

When you study accepted interpretations, one way to learn them is to organize the cards by number. As you compare one card to other cards that share the same number, you will get a sense of how numeric descriptions overlap even when their suit descriptions are different. For example, one attribute linked with the number seven is investigation to enhance clarity. The following is a brief hypothetical model for looking at this same symbolic quality in relation to all the cards that share this number:

- The Seven of Cups: An investigation of a lover's secret outings.
- The Seven of Swords: Examining (investigating) the validity of a contract.
- The Seven of Wands: Exploring (investigating) fantasy versus truth.
- The Seven of Pentacles: The analysis (investigation) of your finances.
- The Chariot (major card 7): Searching (investigating) the right path.
- The Tower (major card 16: 1 + 6 = 7). Scrutiny (the investigation) of a conflict.

This example is specifically focused on only one concept linked with the number seven, investigation. Seven has other attributes, (such as listening to your intuition more attentively), and these qualities will take somewhat different yet related forms when discussing each identically numbered card.

A Tip to Learn Card Meanings

Take time to learn the symbolic meaning of numbers. Numbers repeat themselves through the deck. If you know qualities linked with each number, one through nine, you can use comparable numeric properties to discuss each card that shares the same number. Simply adjust your comments to include the attributes related to each suit or Major Arcana archetype.

Even if you haven't studied numerology or don't believe in it, we offer you the opportunity to learn a little something about the qualities that are said to go with each number. And you can see how we apply these meanings to the various cards. Earlier in this book when we discussed using the cards to do representational readings, you were advised not to worry about learning others' descriptions of these cards. We stand by this advice. However, if you want to learn about card descriptions, you can use this information in conjunction with your personal associations to the images and explore possibilities for how it might be used in your work.

Also, since numeric qualities can differ somewhat when a card is discussed in relation to its suit, our best advice for learning correlations to the minor cards is to have faith in your ability to understand the most important signs and symbols in a card. Trust that you will make up your own mind about their right message in the moment, and enjoy your time playing with them.

Divinatory Meanings

The Aces
Shares Numeric Energy with the Magician, The Wheel of Fortune, and The Sun

In one sense, the Ace means the beginning of something new. It exists like a tiny seed that has the potential to grow into a mighty tree. On the other hand the Ace can signify the best, the most capable, as in someone who can "ace" a test, or be number one in a sport, or be the first to finish a project. However, this meaning can get distorted into prideful arrogance when someone thinks of themselves as "being number one" and more capable than others, whether it's true or not.

A sense of empowerment often goes along with doing something for the first time. Usually no one will argue about the excitement of their first bite of a new taste or their first kiss. No matter how old someone is, people always remember their first time making love. Perhaps you've heard the old heart-touching song about the "first time I saw Paris!" High energy, excitement, creative self-expression and wonder often accompany this number. Because one stands alone as being the first, it can represent the initial step on a path of learning a new skill, starting a new relationship or business, self-discovery, the dawn of awakening, or embarking on a spiritual journey to the realization of one's inner light and love.

Keyword Suggestions for the Symbolism of Number One
- Viewing a new potential, planting seeds
- The start of a new venture or one soon to begin
- Taking the first steps, an original viewpoint
- Initial exuberance, a fresh perspective
- A pioneering spirit, the birthing of possibility
- Being innovative, the first insight

The Ace in Each Suit
Ace of Swords
Linked with the Element Air
and the Initiating Power of Ideas
- Thought coming into existence, original thinking
- The zeal of initial clarity
- Starting an intellectual project or process
- Becoming attracted to a new idea or perspective
- Direct awareness of a new situation

Ace of Wands
Linked with the Element Fire
and the Igniting Power of Passion
- The passionate sparks of creativity
- Feeling a heated desire to pursue something new
- Taking the first step on a soul-illuminating journey
- Awakening the power of your will
- Seeing something in a way that "changes everything"

Ace of Cups
Linked with the Element Water
and The Initial Flow of Emotions
- Fertilizing emotions with desire
- Opening the heart to new possibilities
- Initiating romance
- Learning to open the inner eye of intuition
- Drawing fresh insight from the depths of your subconscious

Ace of Pentacles
Linked with the Element Earth
and Awakening The Power of The Will
- Discovering the strength of your determination
- Starting a money-making or career project
- Planting the seed of desire in physical reality
- Laying the foundation for successful enterprise
- Fertility, whether literal or figurative

The Twos

Shares Numeric Energy with
The High Priestess, Justice, and Judgment

Two is the number of reflection, and the mirroring of inspiration and truth. It can signal coupling, or coming together such as two lovers with hearts entwined, two people engaged in a common project, or one person's ability to intuitively feel what is in the heart and mind of the other. It points to the potential for a relationship or the first stages of one in which each person honors the other's uniqueness and individuality.

Metaphorically, it also indicates the life-giving stage in an undertaking when a seed has already been planted and is being watered, but has not yet begun to sprout above the ground. It can illuminate polarities or clarify the creative tension of the union of opposites, as something original strives to break forth beyond its original boundaries. It is a number that embraces receptivity and the gathering of information or pivotal resources needed to get things going. By contrast, twos can represent splitting apart, and strong emotions and people set against one another, with each trying to win a power struggle while unwilling to hear the other's needs and feelings.

Keyword Suggestions
for the Symbolism of Number Two

- One on one relation, reflections of another
- The nature of duality; opposite or parallel paths
- Polarities such as up/down, waxing/waning, like/dislike
- The two sides of a coin (or story)
- Early on/near the beginning; secondary stages
- Choices, questioning your sole/soul purpose

The Two in Each Suit

Two of Swords
Linked with the Element Air and Reflecting Power of Ideas
- The action/reaction to an intellectual demand or suggestion
- Making a sound effort to actively communicate
- Engaging another to brainstorm possibilities
- Receptivity to or competitiveness with another's idea
- Recognizing or refusing two possibilities and needing to chose
- Blind to seeing or deaf to hearing something important

Two of Wands
Linked with the Element Fire and Activating Desire
- Developing confidence or willpower
- Organizing plans to move toward a goal
- Sensing what choice to make
- Realizing your options
- Focusing fiery intentions

Two of Cups
*Linked with the Element Water
and the Stimulating Flow of Emotions*
- Drinking from the cup of love
- Strengthening trust
- Taking a secondary step toward intimacy or heart's healing
- Choosing between two romantic directions
- Fertilizing a planted seed of passion

Two of Pentacles
Linked with the Element Earth and Motivating Efforts
- Deciding between two careers or money-making options
- Understanding the work needed to get a venture off the ground
- Clarifying expectations or formulating career or project plans
- Acting on a decision
- Considering options or a desired change

The Threes
Shares Numeric Energy with the
Empress, The Hanged Man, and The World

The three brings expansion to the dimensions and qualities of the twos. It is the child of the marriage of one plus two that points to integration, resolution of polarities, letting go of opposition, boldness, and positive developments. Metaphorically it is like the moment when a seed that has been planted, watered, and fertilized breaks through topsoil and its first green shoots or leaves are visible. It tends to signal good times, inspiration, enjoyment and fertile abundance. It's a worldly manifestation comparable to a cluster of three people who are working together and listening to each other's views to further understanding and ambitions. As a number compared in the *Vedas* to the Guru or "a remover of darkness," it points to the expansion of knowledge and serves as a sign of good fortune. As energy begins to rise, careful planning is wise. It may also mean that letting go of old habits or undertakings is needed to open space for new growth.

Three is also a number of confidence and commitment to complete the task at hand. It illuminates recognition of the importance of humility, and respect for the earth with its land, skies, and waters that are essential to all human undertakings, be they mundane or mystical.

Keyword Suggestions
for the Symbolism of Number Three
- Expansiveness, creativity, growth
- Nurturing growth; ambitious efforts
- Mobilizing positive action for accomplishment
- Cultivating sprouted seeds of potential, optimism
- Mentally youthful efforts, triangular relations
- Working cooperatively with others

The Three in Each Suit
Three of Swords
Linked with the Element Air
and the Expanding Power of Ideas
- Introspection and insights
- Cutting through impasse or difficulty
- Envisioning or internalizing an awareness of success
- Bonding with truth on a deeper level
- Using ideas to liberate and empower
- Judicious doubt and skepticism can lead to better plans

Three of Wands
Linked with the Element Fire
and Stimulating Flames of Desire
- Taking action that inspires better opportunity
- Releasing blocks and uncovering inner wisdom
- Fiery passion furthers a sense of purpose
- Directing energy to find resolution
- Creativity enhances a situation

Three of Cups
Linked with the Element Water
and the Evolving Wisdom of Emotions
- A positive flow of emotions ignites trust, opening the heart
- Sensuality, the delights of love, giving and receiving
- A romantic triangle or working through three-way circumstance
- The third eye opens bringing clarity to intuitive insights
- Friendship, fellowship, and the fullness life can offer

Three of Pentacles
Linked with the Element Earth and the Acceleration of Purpose
- Establishing firm earthly connections, being supported
- Personal growth empowers visible momentum of endeavors
- Receiving guidance for healing the physical body
- Creating systematical plans to advance
- Grounding intentions by taking concrete actions
- Developing a habit of careful craftsmanship

The Fours
Shares Numeric Energy with The Emperor and Death
Four is linked with insights that inspire and the impetus to bring change, even when there is stability. When something normally fixed faces the notion of changeability, a sense of security is needed for a person to be willing to envision something better in the future and to be willing to work toward greater future accomplishment. Perhaps this is why this number is often related to building a physical foundation under your dreams, and getting a job well begun.

When it is time to move ahead, "steady progress" is usually the watchword. If you lock yourself into old habits and ways of thinking you may have to break out of them and think anew to enliven your prospects for success. The impetus to grow is unrelenting, like a healthy sprouting vine that brings opportunities to climb higher toward loftier philosophies. Shedding dead weight of the past, either physically or emotionally might just bring greater peace of mind. But reform is not necessary if your tendency toward soul progress leaves you aware of what is going on in and around you, and you know that your real security lies within.

Keyword Suggestions
for the Symbolism of Number Four
- Organizing the building blocks of your success
- Steadfast work to create value, security, and stability
- Self-exploration; deeper understanding of commitments
- Securing intentions to turn your dreams into reality
- Meeting circumstance head on, thinking outside the norm
- Rebelliously sitting on the four-sided square of your creativity

The Four In Each Suit

Four of Swords
Linked with the Element Air
and the Architectural Power of Ideas
- Seeing through deception, clarity of ideas
- Meditation, deep contemplation, or reflection
- Taking time for your self to regroup or clarify purpose
- Becoming more conscious of your truth and destination
- Resistance to outside authority; rethinking plans

Four of Wands
Linked with the Element Fire and Willful Pursuits
- Excited efforts to claim or reclaim your joy and/or power
- Using social networking to advance personal boundaries
- Celebration of previous work and recharging motives
- Favorable exchanges that inspire achievement
- A solid foundation balances innovative enterprise

Four of Cups
Linked with the Element Water and Emotional Reflection
- Searching for what makes your heart happy
- Past emotional toxins interfere with opening your heart
- Questioning emotional integrity
- Personal assessment; questioning relationships
- Wanting to change present circumstances

Four of Pentacles
Linked with the Element Earth and Organization of Efforts
- The importance of your material world, property, the home
- Organizing a plan to get ahead and increase finances
- Laying a strong foundation in order to fulfill dreams/ambitions
- Grounding your finances in heart-felt choices
- Developing tangible, skilled craftsmanship in your work

The Fives

Shares Numeric Energy with High Priest (Heirophant) and Temperance

Five often involves quick thinking, mental flexibility, wit, and communication. This numeric vibration possesses a youthful vigor, and likes to move either up or down, backward or forwards, but it doesn't like to stand still. Because of its verve, it's willing to give a needed push to get things moving. This may involve letting go of a false self-conception to discover a deeper truth, or focusing attention on improving clarity of perceptions. It also challenges narrow-mindedness and inspires taking a deeper look at life, as its catchphrase is "It's time to grow!"

In relationships, a five is sometimes a red arrow that points to communication problems in which someone (or everyone) is not hearing the other(s) well. Or one person insists on having his or her own way rather than respecting the need for mutual give-and-take. If the relationship is to endure or improve, conscious work on understanding each other better may be needed. To achieve success and move forward, challenges must be met and overcome in order to move along on the road to harmony and more accurate perceptions.

Keyword Suggestions for the Symbolism of Number Five

- Nurturing projects in the mid stages of growth
- Seeing results of developing potentials
- Experiencing deeper levels of communication
- Walking the middle path
- Using common sense that fosters personal evolution
- Facing challenging aspects of romantic or working relations

The Five in Each Suit

Five of Swords
Linked with the Element Air and Provocative Ideas
- Nervous intelligence; looking over your shoulder
- Offensive/defensive competitive tactics
- Being consumed by ideas or concerns
- Spirited thinking, changing your mind
- Seeking and/or speaking your needs and impressions

Five of Wands
Linked with the Element Fire and the Fiery Spirit of Will
- Love of adventure or risk
- Energetic, bold attempts to overcome difficulties
- Demands on time create a need to focus on priorities
- Meeting the challenge of competition and working to be triumphant
- Working to overcome unnecessary stress

Five of Cups
Linked with the Element Water and The Swift Flow of Emotion
- Tender hearted feelings meet Godzilla
- Vulnerable sensitivities need to be addressed
- Lost in the labyrinth of love
- Letting desires and hopes interfere with realistic perception
- Obsession with what has been lost instead of living in the present

Five of Pentacles
Linked with the Element Earth and the Exploration of Potentials
- Questioning the value of material dreams
- Needing to feel more secure or grounded
- Concerns involving the home or material property
- Challenges regarding work or finances

The Sixes

Shares Numeric Energy with The Lovers and The Devil

The numeric vibration of six is usually auspicious and often a sign to enjoy the moment. It points to good feelings and appreciation for the gift of life. This may be in the realm of clarity of mind, sexuality, sensuality, or other physical pleasures. It's also a reminder that life is filled with many possibilities, and that we're more likely to benefit when we swim with the waves of life rather than struggle against them.

Sixes can herald opening the heart, unraveling complicated feelings, seductive experiences, amorous opportunities, and even heightened perspectives and profound visions. Also, it is a number of compromise, or a victory or breakthrough in resolving a conflict of interest. It is associated with a harmonious energy that encourages working with others to find mutually acceptable paths and agreements rather than persisting in opposition.

In the Kabbalah, six represents beauty. As such, it reminds us to be alert to the splendor in tiny objects as well as sweeping landscapes lit by the celestial light of the rising or setting sun, and to contribute our compassion whenever and however we can—whether inwardly or outwardly, in our relationships and the physical world.

Keyword Suggestions for
the Symbolism of Number Six

- Love and/or making commitments
- Equal measures bring balance and harmony
- Balancing opposites, overcoming ambivalence
- Intuitive inspiration
- Personal growth or taking steps toward achievement
- Connecting with important people or social causes
- Building a better reality

The Six in Each Suit

Six of Swords
Linked with the Element Air and Unifying Ideas
- Understanding which choices to make
- Paying attention to your own preferences and intentions
- Wise decision making releases blocks and inspires hope
- Watching the rise and fall of thoughts with detached acceptance
- A clear, balanced mind replaces confusion

Six of Wands
Linked with the Element Fire and Energetic Transitions
- Jumping into an opportunity stimulates action
- Achieving inner/outer balance
- Conversing with fiery people sparks awareness
- Creativity crafts practical solutions.
- Victory over self-generated stumbling blocks

Six of Cups
Linked with the Element Water and the Gentle Nature of Sensuality
- The momentum of good energy; feeling valued
- Taking action to increase harmony
- Passionate feelings; to touch and be touched on a deep level
- Listening to the heart and relating to others in a meaningful way
- Intimate and beautiful lovemaking

Six of Pentacles
Linked with the Element Earth and Grounded, Focused Efforts
- Creativity invokes practical solutions
- Promoting ideas to attract financial success
- Engaging partnerships to open the door to greater fortune
- Striving for abundance and vitality
- Giving or receiving something of tangible value

The Sevens

Shares Numeric Energy with The Chariot and The Tower

It has been said that life well lived is an alternation of action and rest, of moving in a direction and then pausing to reflect on which direction to move next. Seven combines these qualities. It is a card of action in the world, and of pausing to assess the results of those actions.

Also, seven is the number of mysticism, dreams, intuition, and following psychic avenues. By contrast, it may indicate needing to pull yourself out of the fog and become more grounded. It's your task to discern what practical actions to take now. It's no surprise, then, that when under the sway of a seven, consulting your dreams, penning a poem, or giving a bouquet of roses to the one who attracts your heart may seem very practical indeed.

Seven is widely considered to be lucky. Yet at the same time, it is also considered a number of uncertainty, secrets, and the potential investigation of both choices and the unknown. You may have to choose among several desirable alternatives, or several undesirable ones—and then live with the consequences of choosing one or another of your options. Your patience will help you best juggle options and know where the fog of ambiguity lifts. Once you clearly see your direction, you can arrive where you need to be. Staying "under the radar" or keeping information to yourself that could cause trouble for you or others may be wise.

**Keyword Suggestions
for the Symbolism of Number Seven**
• Juggling spiritual and worldly values
• Self-discovery leads to purposeful choices
• Learning to use your intuitive or healing powers
• Trusting your imagination and creative visions
• Finding a healing path for your mind, body, and emotions
• Overcoming ambivalence heightens your sense of self
• Choosing among several apparently positive possibilities

The Seven in Each Suit

Seven of Swords

Linked with the Element Air
and the Mystifying Power of Ideas

- Sorting through uncertainty
- Gaining mastery of occult or spiritual knowledge
- Explaining or asserting unorthodox ideas
- Using the sword of discrimination to conquer fears or doubts
- Avoiding doing something that could incite trouble

Seven of Wands

Linked with the Element Fire
and The Secret Heart of Passion

- Breaking ties with false ideas, empty promise, or fake friends
- Being motivated to guide others with your passion or compassion
- Fantasy stirs desire for adventure or a life style beyond the norm
- Combining imagination with enduring efforts to succeed
- Finding resolve despite difficulties

Seven of Cups

Linked with the Element Water
and Overflowing Rivers of Desire

- Gluttony for pleasure; lust; flirtatiousness
- Using emotions to write poetry, songs, or art
- Working with your intuition or doing healing arts
- Confusion or getting lost in disturbing emotional circumstance
- Juggling dependency and independence while keeping your individuality

Seven of Pentacles

Linked with the Element Earth
and the Power to Grasp Your Dreams

- Marketing your ideas and overcoming financial stress
- Making concrete efforts to improve investment skills
- Gambling or risk taking to increase your worldly fortune
- Security versus adventure that might hold greater rewards
- Being lifted on wings of spirit while anchored in matter

The Eights

Shares Numeric Energy with Strength and The Star

An eight is an infinity symbol standing on its end. As such, its possible implications are limitless. Widely used meanings include values such as discipline, setting limits, integrity, honesty and truth, seriousness, organization and responsibility. Eight can represent difficulty, and also the luck, knowledge, and ability to move through and beyond it. Linked with the laser focus that can bring mastery of a craft, it includes knowing how to do something well even when obstacles arise.

Assuming the responsibility of being your own authority as you make your choices plays a strong role in the personal empowerment that some equate with this number. It can also, however, represent the wisdom to understand limits set by others as well as determination to enjoy life despite them. Also allied with the power to descend into previously unexplored chambers of your mind, it can herald awakening to greater order, peace, and insight.

By journeying to another place, whether in the outer world or within yourself, you may find alternatives to what you have always thought of as certainties. The eight reminds you that your own thoughts, words, and actions weigh heavily in what happens to you and in you. Such perceptions become part of your path to experiential wisdom where you acquire a broader and deeper understanding of yourself and your own soul purpose beyond all instructions given by society. A key to this knowledge is asking yourself what you yourself truly value most.

Keyword Suggestions
for the Symbolism of Number Eight

- Focused energy that can get results
- Noticing habitual mental patterns that need to be improved
- Questioning whether you want to take responsibility or commitment
- Personal empowerment and improvement become priorities
- Increased awareness of higher values
- Courage that enables you to win out against greater forces

The Eight in Each Suit

Eight of Swords
Linked with the Element Air and Intensifying Ideas
- Undertaking a daily meditative practice to clear your mind.
- Taking blame or feeling responsibility for a problematic situation
- Worries, sorrow, or frustrations create anxiety
- Breaking through old ideas to improve complicated entanglements.
- Finding energy to burst through self-imposed barriers

Eight of Wands
Linked with the Element Fire and Strength of Will
- Intense focus on priorities
- Heated desires turn thinking into actions
- Striving for personal gain from creative efforts
- Anger, mistrust, or lack of communication
- Finding strength to overcome obstacles or energize your commitments

Eight of Cups
Linked with the Element Water and Balance of Emotions
- Seeking stability in uncertain emotional relations
- Jealousy, fear of betrayal or loss
- Masking regrets or heavy concerns or hiding true feelings
- Hearing gossip about your life or gossiping about others
- Using intuition in uncharted territory

Eight of Pentacles
*Linked with the Element Earth
and Gaining Material Success*
- Working hard for accolades
- Overcoming moneymaking or financial challenges
- Seeing tangible results of focused efforts
- Applying your talents to reach creative or financial goals
- Gaining greater mastery in your chosen craft

The Nines

Shares Numeric Energy with The Hermit and The Moon

The energetic nines, the last of the single digit numbers, are linked with endings, completion, the tipping point of a cycle, and resolution. They can be compared with the moment near the finish line of a race or the deadline of a project, where you can get a second wind and draw on an extra reserve of energy to come in first, or at least be able to finish. Or perhaps you don't have to exert extra energy to bring a matter to completion, but rather it's a time for awareness, reflection, and minor adjustments, like an artist looking at a painting or a sculptor at a statute, taking stock of which final touches will make it turn out just right.

Because this numeric vibration is linked with the mystic, the sensitive, and the psychic, it might even refer to a teacher or guru-stimulating realizations that transcend conventional reason and bring great insight. Consequently, the positive aspects of nine can combine the best of spiritual and worldly inclinations to lead to self-mastery and profound shifts in perspective.

But nine energies can also bring you face to face with the challenges of your mental and emotional life. Meeting these well can open a door to the next stage in your personal evolution. This encourages the combination of looking and reaching into and outside your self to find the willpower to get through tough times. As you strive to reach for success, your goals crystallize into a final or nearly final form that enlivens your commitment and engaging lifestyle.

Keyword Suggestions
for the Symbolism of Number Nine

- The master, guru, the mystic, or elusive wise person
- Lighting the lamp of timeless wisdom
- Seeking a mystical or soul path to liberation
- Independence, solitude, withdrawing from the superficial
- Forceful actions or reactions; owning your power
- A guiding force that illuminates integrity and clarity
- Ending one cycle or journey; beginning another
- Letting go of attachments or misunderstandings; moving on

The Nine in Each Suit

Nine of Swords
Linked with the Element Air
and the Revolving Gateway of Ideas
- Over-thinking situations
- Getting wrapped-up in feeling powerless or other frustrations
- Looking logically at resolving issues
- Feeling chained or threatened by circumstances
- Excessive worry, whether about real misfortune or something you create in your mind

Nine of Wands
Linked with the Element Fire and Making Commitments
- Coping with a challenging or hot situation
- Mistrust of communications
- Assertively stating your stance
- Heated transformational change
- Motivation becomes action to realize your desires

Nine of Cups
Linked with the Element Water
and the Flow of Emotional Change
- Intense emotional communications
- Questioning trust and detaching from expectations
- Diving under the surface to find the truth of the heart
- Listening to your intuition in regards to future decisions
- Meeting new people or joining an on-line dating service

Nine of Pentacles
Linked with the Element Earth and Renewing Forces of Life
- Adopting a winning attitude over financial obstacles
- Enjoyment of earthly passions
- Taking concrete steps to acquire tangible property
- Gratitude for the blessings in the garden of your life
- Approaching attainment of your financial or material goals

The Tens

Shares Numeric Energy with The Magician, The Wheel of Fortune, and The Sun

When doing numerology, the ten returns to a number one vibration (1 + 0 = 1). It reflects changing perspectives and the potential for new beginnings. Seeds previously sown through earlier efforts have yielded certain results. You may experience the completion of a cycle or begin to lay plans for a new path. Now is the moment for rethinking or reorganizing methods necessary for reaching a goal, or visualizing better prospects for how you want to move forward. This is often a time to recharge your energy, stay positive, and look realistically at your hopes and dreams.

Because effort over an extended period on any path in life is often filled with ups and downs, idealisms and perfectionism may need to be exchanged for acceptance of what life offers. This applies in the physical (Pentacles), emotional (Cups), mental (Swords), or spiritual (Wands) realms. This circumstance doesn't have to be looked at as right or wrong, but just what is. Taking time to pause, reflect, and also to ask yourself what you truly want enhances clarity of purpose.

Even if the situation you are looking at appears negative or you are dreading the ending of a cycle, this number points to the potential for moving toward new or renewed beginnings, breaking ties with old habits, or learning something of value from your past. It can be a reminder that if you play your cards right, better things lie ahead, you still have time to win. A dark moment is just a moment and if you can remember to metaphorically light a candle, more reflections of light will illuminate your life.

Keyword Suggestions
for the Symbolism of Number Ten
- Initial understanding of an underlying truth
- Having an "ah-ha!" moment
- Returning to a place or situation, starting anew
- Expanded dimensions of the familiar
- Reviewing intentions and reconsidering choices or decisions
- Overcoming fears
- Transformation to a higher level of consciousness

The Ten in Each Suit

Ten of Swords
Linked with the Element Air
and the Regenerative Power of Ideas
- Detaching from draining ideas or worries
- Seeking mental stimulation; healing, or freedom from negativity
- The need to get out of your head into greater aliveness
- Winds of change brings renewal of potentials
- Tapping into transcendent consciousness

Ten of Wands
Linked with the Element Fire and Magnetic Passion
- Jumping over hurdles toward your desires
- Recognizing a finishing point, seeing light at the end of a tunnel
- Sifting through smoldering ash of the past to gain understanding
- Letting go, and coming to terms with life lessons
- Tapping into transcendent consciousness

Ten of Cups
Linked with the Element Water and Clarifying Truth
- Learning to trust anew
- Being comfortable within your emotional body
- Facing a new start or romance with hope and optimism
- Opening or expanding your intuitive perceptions
- Communications heal heavy-hearted moodiness or stagnation
- Finding beauty and joy in romance or dating/mating

Ten of Pentacles
Linked with the Element Earth and Walking On Solid Ground
- Taking tangible fresh steps toward gaining success
- Creating the reality of your own money making visions
- Using practical resources to build a better world
- Recognizing priorities and how to best use your time
- Working to heal Mother Earth.

At this point, we've come to the end of our conversation about numbers and the Minor Arcana. It's time to step into the world of royalty and look at the next group of cards in the deck, the face cards or court cards. Onward!

15.

THE COURT CARDS: REFLECTIONS ON THE ROYALS

In Medieval and Renaissance times the nobility ran society (along with the Roman Catholic Church in much of Europe). Since the earliest known Tarot cards were created in that era, the court cards reflected the social structure of the times. Today the cards point to noble characteristics, regal values, imperial motives, and great strength. Since court cards characterize extraordinary people, you can compare them to personalities you know to help you understand their unique characteristics. Pages are said to represent questioning youth, knights are crusaders of soulful pursuits, queens correspond to the feminine controlling voice of sometimes wise and sometimes hard-hearted counsel, and the king is the dominating, energetic masculine force of reason or oppression.

In relation to the four elements and the qualities each represents, some court cards are more penetrating in their intellect (Swords); some are more intuitive, emotional, and romantic, (Cups); some are more passionate, flirtatious, and given to attracting the admiring eyes of the court (Wands); and, some are more concerned with the realm's productivity and tangible wealth (Pentacles), but all are consumed with living life to the fullest.

When studying the court cards, take a few moments and identify with each one at a time to become better acquainted with their symbolic qualities. Whatever a card's gender, which of its features do you recognize as most developed within yourself? Which others would you like to put your efforts into developing in order to succeed in walking the royal road to satisfaction? You might also want to consider which qualities are most attractive or repulsive to you. How do you connect with, embody, or disown the majestic or offensive qualities of the court card personalities?

The Court Cards
Correspondences for the Cards of Nobility
The key words on this chart can be viewed as real or metaphorical; internalized or externalized.

Social Role

KING	QUEEN	KNIGHT	PAGE
Masculine authority	Feminine authority	Control	Testing limits
Commanding	Nourishing	Charging forth	Learning
Achievement	Dominance	Action	Finding identity
Scrutinizing	Placating	Searching	Texting
Logical	Interpersonally sensitive	Asserting	Discovering

The Pages

The four Pages point to a person in the stage of learning something, whether it is conceptual knowledge, love's lessons, or other explorations. They are the personification of youth, or sometimes inquisitive older people, who are developing a skill in some craft, business, or other work that augments their sense of personal power or earning potential. A page might also point to learning about oneself or how to handle relationships, or the importance of spending time with people who open doors to more expansive activities, greater self knowledge, and potential fulfillment.

Ideally, a page reads and listens to materials that tell how to be effective in what he or she wants to do. The page watches others do those things well, draws out suggestions and comments, and eventually moves beyond the stage of a page into that of a journeyman or knight. Pursuing a path of dreams, ultimately he or she becomes an expert at climbing the ladder of success. This can be as important for a mature person developing new expertise as for a youth beginning his or her adult journey.

A page's immaturity can get in his or her way and there can be a problem with self-perception. Huge numbers of young people who know little about life think they know everything. As unseasoned pseudo-experts, they may be pure at heart, but don't realize that there is so much to be learned.

It's not only young people who can awkwardly stumble when climbing the ladder toward both worldly and self-knowledge. We all have things to learn at different stages in our life. Even elders can play the page's role as they learn to explore life anew while navigating the surprising twists and turns of old age.

A less responsible page of any age may represent the person who is less emotionally mature and doesn't take responsibility for following through on decisions, actions, or commitments.

If you're still trying to understand the meaning of the page, replace the word with "apprentice," or "student," which are more widely used contemporary terms that don't have the implications of subservience that go with "page." Imagine the mind opening excitedly to noble possibilities, and you will be in touch with the vibrant, lofty energy of this active force.

Keyword Suggestions for the Pages
- Inexperienced, yet willful pursuit of leadership
- Getting in touch with your personal power
- Taking greater responsibilities
- Innocent lack of wisdom, naiveté
- Questioning the character of one's female or male role or purpose
- Learning one's sense of worth
- Action in hope of gaining admiration or advantage

The Page in Each Suit
The Page of Swords
Linked with the Element Air and Youthful, Untried Ideas
- Moving into new realms of understanding
- Learning to perceive clearly what's happening around you
- Honoring and defining your inner truth
- Experimenting with your personal power

The Page of Wands
Linked with the Element Fire and Turning up the Flame
- Acting without thinking about the consequences
- Rethinking your creativity or making it an important part of life
- Making a commitment not to give up on attaining your goals
- Vigorous but possibly immature communication
- Flirtatiousness and sexual play color many endeavors

The Page of Cups
Linked with the Element Water and Lessons on Opening the Heart
- Testing the boundaries of love or what moves the heart
- Gaining experience in intimate courtship
- Getting easily caught in the grip of Eros and emotion
- Becoming more sensitive to intuitive energy

The Page of Pentacles
Linked with the Element Earth and Career Potency
- Developing working plans or taking them to a new level
- Becoming an important figure in your career or community
- Juggling play and work, silliness and wisdom
- Learning to trust and use your ideas in the business world

The Knights

Historically, the Knight is typically envisioned as armed, armored, and ready for battle. In modern times, however, there are many gentler, and more thoughtful, and often more useful and appropriate forms of "warrior" energy. For instance, even though the knight is a symbol of male domination with status and cachet, today many people can see beyond that chapter of history and applaud the "anima" (feminine) qualities in the knight. This changing portrayal is essential in this age when women are joining the armed services and asserting their place as equal to men in the society.

Boldness, courage, perseverance in achieving goals, and strength are most often the internal structure inside a knight's armor. On the other hand, this image can also indicate that someone is emotionally armored and chronically tense, or just the opposite, so drunk on love that they go beyond the norm to romantically pursue the person of their desire (or their creative love and vision). The knight goes forward without fear to compete with an intellectual spear, seldom doubting his or her mission.

Modern knight energy is also linked with those who have grand strategies to defeat others who are less powerful. The struggle to be better than "satisfactory" is widespread in middle-management personnel who do not make the big decisions but carry out the orders of the Board of Directors and top executives. Yet there is also the romantic "knight in shining armor" who lives for protecting a maiden in distress. And there are those knights who swear allegiance to a great cause and are loyal to doing heroic deeds and of being of service to others.

Since knights can also represent sons, brothers, uncles, and male cousins, boyfriends, or lovers, you might want to consider who the knight on your card represents to you. Is there something that needs to be dealt with in regard to someone who is symbolized by the knight in your or your querent's life? Are you carrying around such a person in your mind or emotions? Has an attractive or powerful person come gallantly into your life, or are you on a path to develop those qualities in yourself?

Keyword Suggestions for the Knights
- Owning your own power and courage
- Using your influence to make change
- Assertively moving toward a goal
- Becoming strongly identified with a motivating strategy
- Being invited into a community of noble thinkers
- Going on an emotional, financial, or spiritual crusade
- Being willing to battle for something you value
- A person of stature challenges or affects your progress

The Knight in Each Suit

The Knight of Swords
Linked with the Element Air and Asserting Ideas
- Learning to replace negative with positive ideas
- Noble ideas attract or inspire the mind
- Standing centered and strong in your beliefs
- Overcoming limits and empowering your confidence to win

The Knight of Wands
Linked with the Element Fire
and Heated Passion of Pursuits
- Being willing to explore possibilities outside normal boundaries
- Forcefully asserting your independence or get-up-and-go energy
- Feeling your power and passion and pursuing your ambitions
- Heroically being willing to work or even fight for what you believe

The Knight of Cups
Linked with the Element Water and Valiant Emotions
- An intuitive or romantic person triggers a waterfall of emotions
- Seeking opportunities for romance, flirtatious playfulness, or sex
- Competitive energy enters an emotional situation
- Courageously coming to someone's emotional rescue or sweeping them off their feet—or getting swept off yours

The Knight of Pentacles
Linked with the Element Earth
and Pursuing Worldly Ambitions
- Striving fiercely to win pursuits connected with money and power
- Taking control of disquieting group situations
- Meeting, overcoming, and commanding earthly challenges
- Mounting the steed of courage to gain results, awards, or honor
- Working or fighting to protect the natural environment

The Queens

A true queen is a woman of power rather than merely a consort for the king. She is often also a woman of glamour, for she has the finest dressmakers, jewelers, and cosmeticians in the realm to help her appear to be the fairest of them all. In this matter, for the most part today's entertainment divas are more queenly than many female politicians and executive businesswomen who can also be favorably represented by this card, and this sovereign archetype.

Many "queens" of whatever kind, however, get so hypnotized by the hype around their fame, fortune, and reputation that they pay little attention to developing their inner qualities. Like a king, a queen may be kind or cruel, compassionate or hard-hearted. She may have become queen through a marriage that united kingdoms or families of great wealth, and if so, she was probably as well trained in the art of exercising power as the king. Often enough, a queen may thoughtfully influence the king, and hers may be the true power and intellect that shapes the policies that run their realm. Drawing on her soft virtues and the subtleties of feminine intuition she may be even more skilled than the king at the intricate nuances of sensing the motives of others and engaging those around her to serve her will. Most likely she understands well that those whom she helps in their endeavors will in turn be more inclined to help her in her own.

When a woman possesses the power of nobility and also the nurturing qualities of a mother, such as the late Princess Diana of Great Britain who was in line to become the queen, she is likely to be seen as a natural leader. Strong women who use their power effectively will probably also have prominent duties and become publicly recognized for their work and socially valuable pursuits.

Keyword Suggestions for the Queen

- A confident woman who is strong in her world
- Feminine power, authority, or leadership
- Directing ambitions toward success
- Enriching other's lives through heartfelt wisdom and nurturing
- A regal sense of importance in decision-making
- Dominance, determination and action over passivity
- Using resources wisely to construct castles of victory

The Queen in Each Suit
The Queen of Swords
Linked with the Element Air and Empowering Ideas
- Organizing systems of thoughts
- Accelerating the momentum of ideas
- Effectively balancing the analytical mind and emotions
- Clarity of vision and sense of direction overcomes ambiguities
- Building intellectual fortresses to fulfill higher purposes

The Queen of Wands
Linked with the Element Fire and Consummation of Passion
- Achieving goals by will directed with confidence
- Receptive mirroring of creative masculine consciousness
- Directing a successful enterprise
- A strong, fiery woman who doesn't take "no" for an answer

The Queen of Cups
Linked with the Element Water and Control of Emotions
- Wife/nurturer/lover who drinks from her cup of passion
- Queen of hearts who trumps selfish or uncaring motives
- Embracing trust and noble virtues
- Deeply loyal and committed love
- Using intuition to see what is coming and expand understanding

The Queen of Pentacles
Linked with the Element Earth and Worldly Leadership
- Enjoying the harvest of career activities
- Advocating financial possibilities with a commanding hand
- Building bridges with respectful communication
- Enjoying nature; using natural resources wisely for the good of all
- Fertile ideas and seeing results of creative endeavors

The Kings

Kings embody and symbolize wealth and power. Some are compassionate, kind, or wise. Others are the opposite. Historically, many kings gained the throne through ruthlessness, duplicity, and crushing anyone who got in their way. In today's world, a chief executive officer, movie star, or politician can be a contemporary incarnation of a "king."

Once at the top of the regal ladder, the king has more room to maneuver than when he held a lower station. As a result, his true personality and inclinations are more likely to show. Generous or greedy, kind or cruel, the parts he played during his ascent may fade into the shadows, unless the masks he wore are glued on so tight that he sees the roles he plays as his true self. There are kings who act like those who came before them, and others who chart their own way and become truly themselves, such as a Marcus Aurelius or Charlemagne. Such kings unite their peoples rather than dividing them. They form alliances when they can and resort to conquest only when they must.

A wise king does not jump to conclusions, but listens to the counsel of all sides and interests before coming to a decision. If prudent, he acts in ways that advance the interests of those around him, so that in their gratitude they support him in return. His edicts help his people and kingdom prosper, like an ideal mixture of rain and sun to support the growth of crops.

You might ask yourself which kingly qualities you find attractive, which you loathe, and which you want to cultivate in yourself. When a king is drawn, you might ask whether there is a father, uncle, brother, husband, boyfriend or other male authority figures with whom there is a concern that needs to be addressed.

Keyword Suggestions for the King
- A strong, powerful leader or manager who can be magnetic
- A teacher or mentor who can bring about transformation in others
- Meeting a man who provides opportunities for worldly fulfillment
- Obtaining enough wealth or power to wear a crown of achievement
- Reaching goals after a long period of active effort
- Improving your quality of life by taking a strong stand
- Awakening to an expansive conscious awareness

The King in Each Suit
The King of Swords
Linked with the Element Air
and the Influencing Power of Ideas
- Transformative visions with a higher purpose
- Influencing others with commanding ideas
- Mastering the mind through meditation
- Mentally altering the direction of your life toward greater success

The King of Wands
Linked with the Element Fire and Willful Leadership
- A strong, attractive man with a magnetic, fiery elegance
- Spirited, high masculine energy focused on maximum efficiency
- Getting in touch with soul commitments or weighty agreements
- Cultivating extraordinary abilities or craftsmanship

The King of Cups
Linked with the Element Water and Fulfilling Dreams of Love
- Passionate and charming, a man who understands the art of love
- A seductive lover (or male friend) with emotional charisma
- A sensitive man who wishes intimacy
- Fulfillment of the heart's desire, finding true romance

The King of Pentacles
Linked with the Element Earth and the Mastery of Finances
- Advantageous investments that provide good returns
- Visions of grandeur lead to building palaces of golden success
- Becoming influential in the community, yet keeping grounded
- A compelling leader in your field or the financial world
- Recognizing what is most important to accomplish.

The greatest and most admirable of pages, knights, queens, and kings are those who recall and consistently act on the words of the ancient Greek statesman and leader of Athens, Pericles, who declared, "What you leave behind is not what is engraved in stone monuments, but what is woven into the lives of others."

EPILOGUE

19. *The* SUN

In these pages we have described some of our ways of using Tarot cards. Since everyone lives in their own unique reality, there are many different opinions about the correct or the best way to interpret or use Tarot imagery. The truth is simple: there are diverse perspectives and methods, and always will be. Here we have opened up a few more possibilities. There would be no point in writing this book if our portrayals and methods were the same as those you already know.

Whether you do divinatory readings or use imagery as a therapeutic tool for healing, it's essential to discover how the cards can most effectively enrich your life and the lives of others. In regard to the questions people ask and the problems they face, answer from what you feel in your heart and understand in your mind. Learning all you can about how you can work with the cards to guide a person helps you to do your highest quality work and to be confident of your abilities. As we wrote several years ago in *Tarot d'Amour: Find Love, Sex, and Romance in the Cards* "Your intuition, present awareness, and depth and breadth of vision are the most valuable keys to determining the implication of the cards."

Many of the Tarot images live in the psyche somewhere far beyond the places words can touch. They can throw open the doors to new horizons of possibility. We hope your efforts turn the Wheel of Fortune in the direction of opportunities for abundant success and enjoyment, and that the muses and guardians of the Tarot will be with you on your journey.

APPENDIX 1

Journal Template

My Journal

✏️ Today's Notes

✏️ Date and time of reading:

✏️ Name of person getting reading:

✏️ Age:

✏️ Divinatory or Representational Session:

✏️ What cards were drawn?

✏️ How were they placed on the table?

✏️ What topics were discussed?

✏️ Noteworthy Information discovered during this experience:

✏️ My reaction:

APPENDIX 2

Archetypes Associated with the Major Arcana Cards

In a previous work some years ago, we wrote, "Reflecting on the twenty-two cards of the Major Arcana and their archetypal themes can open your mind to the deeper levels of their messages."[3] Made popular by Carl Jung, the term *archetype refers to universal themes, experiences, or symbolic mental patterns that live in the collective unconscious of all people.* Archetypes are often the objects of our dreams and our waking reality, our myths and fairy tales. Timeless beyond language and race, for the most part they live free from the doctrines of culture, place, and traditions. For example, the archetypes of the father or mother or child are relevant to all people in all times. Depending on the historic age, clothing styles and hairdos may change, but even so, everyone from the far distant past to our present time will understand these concepts.

When we study the psychology of the Tarot, we find that each Major Arcana card is associated with an archetype. For example, the third Major Arcana card, The Empress, is the unconditional light of true love, the nurturing voice of the Mother, the protector and keeper of the seeds of life. She is linked with the Greek goddess Demeter, the celestial wise woman, the feminine principle, and rites of fertility. Her worldly consort, The Emperor, and fourth Major Arcana card, is linked with the Greek god Ares, masculine power, and an archetype associated with the varied roles of the Father: aggressive or peaceful, mentally strong, often authoritative, and willing to assume controlling roles such as the heads of state or leaders of community. By understanding a Tarot image in relation to its archetype, we gain a valuable resource to help us view the images in connection with practical, day-to-day, universal concerns. As you increase your knowledge of the cards, you will probably become sensitive to various ways in which the archetypes can influence your interpretations of their relevance to particular questions and issues. Following is our list of correspondences between the Tarot and archetypes:

CARD NUMBER	CARD NAME	ARCHETYPE
I	The Magician	Trickster
II	The High Priestess	Divine Maiden
III	The Empress	Feminine Leader
IV	The Emperor	Male Authority
V	The High Priest (Hierophant)	Teacher
VI	The Lovers	Marriage/Crossroads
VII	The Chariot	Journey
VIII	Strength	Hero/Heroine
IX	The Hermit	Wise Person
X	Wheel of Fortune	Evolving Destiny or Fate
XI	Justice	Balance and Fairness
XII	The Hanged Man	The Wounded Healer
XIII	Death	Transformation, Rebirth
XIV	Temperance	Virtue, Integrity
XV	The Devil	Temptation
XVI	The Tower	Passage
XVII	The Star	The Guide
XVIII	The Moon	The Intuitive
XIX	The Sun	The Source
XX	Judgment	The Judge
XXI	The World	Home
O	The Fool	The Child

This is not an exhaustive list. It begins the range of possibilities. There are many other archetypes, such as water pouring from a stream or spring that signifies renewal and energy. Other archetypes might come to mind as you view your cards, or perhaps they will appear in your dreams. You may decide that another archetype seems more appropriate for a specific card in connection with a specific person. When discussing card images, it is best to use whatever correspondence makes the most sense to you.

ENDNOTES

Chapter 1

1. Robert Place, *Alchemy and the Tarot* (Saugerties, New York: Hermes Publications, 2011).

2. For the 1506 description of the *atouts,* see Stuart R. Kaplan, *Encyclopedia of Tarot, Vol. 1* (New York: U.S. Games Systems, 1985).

3. Yoav Ben-Dov, *CBD Tarot de Marseille: A Faithful Reproduction of the Traditional Tarot.* Deck (CreateSpace; also Galaxy Tone Software. Israel: www.cbdTarot.com, 2013).

4. A brief clarification of frequently misunderstood terms. *Psychologists* may refer to someone with scientific, therapeutic, or counseling training and generally refers to all professionals involved with the study or treatment of the human mind, including its emotional and its physiological or somatic dimensions. This includes many whose work is primarily scientific who do not see patients or clients at all. *Psychiatrists* are required to have an MD. They may be trained in any of several varieties of psychotherapy. Some rely primarily on prescribing medication. *Psychoanalysts* must be certified by a psychoanalytic training institute. In the US they must hold an MD and be certified to prescribe medication whereas in some countries, individuals with various backgrounds (such as literary or historical) but suitable aptitudes may be accepted into psychoanalytic training programs. *Psychotherapists* include the two groups above and many who are trained in any of a variety of other approaches, such as Person-Centered Therapy, Gestalt Therapy, Existential Therapy, Cognitive Behavior Therapy, etc. If they are not psychiatrists, they typically hold a PhD or PsyD or MA and certification by a training institute and state accrediting agency. *Counselors'* training may very closely resemble that of psychotherapists, not uncommonly with a specialty such as couples counseling or school counseling. Psychologists of whatever kind typically hold a Ph.D. or PsyD or MA or MS in psychology or counseling.

Chapter Three
1. Kurt Lewin, *A dynamic theory of personality* (New York: McGraw-Hill, 1935). See also Kurt Lewin, *Resolving Social Conflicts.* (New York: Harper, 1948).

Chapter Six.
1. *Discourses, 6th ed* (San Francisco: Sufism Reoriented, 1967).
2. Swiss psychiatrist Carl Jung was initially part of Freud's inner circle. He coined the term "complex" and discovered that reaction times to emotionally loaded words were slower than those to neutral words. Eventually he broke away from Freud, whom he considered overly committed to his own theories, and developed "Analytical Psychology." Alfred Adler was more interested in the conscious than the unconscious mind. He and stressed the need to understand people in their social contexts, and the social influences on them. His "Individual Psychology" initiated the Humanistic-existential tradition in psychology.
3. Arthur Rosengarten, *Tarot and Psychology: Spectrums of Possibility* (St. Paul, MN: Paragon House, 2000).

Chapter 7
1. Paraphrased from Fritz Perls, *Ego, Hunger, and Aggression: The Beginning of Gestalt Therapy* (New York: Random House, 1947).
2. Peter Elbow, *Writing Without Teachers* (New York: Oxford University Press, 1998).

Chapter 8
1. We offer our gratitude to the late Ann Teachworth of the New Orleans Gestalt Institute for developing the method adapted to Tarot imagery here and labeled a "spectator spread." At her institute, often she would see a couple together once, then see them individually using what we have labeled the "spectator" approach for as many sessions as needed for their parents to "resolve" their relationship problems, then bring the couple back together. When they came together after having resolved their parents' problems, often their own issues were gone or greatly reduced, too.

Chapter 9

1. Maurice Merleau-Ponty, *The Primacy of Perception* (Evanston, IL: Northwestern University Press 1964).
2. Aaron Beck, *Cognitive Therapy and The Emotional Disorders.* (New York and London: Penguin Meridian, 1979).
3. Bruno Bettelheim, *Freud and Man's Soul: An Important Re-Interpretation of Freud's Theory* (New York: Random House Vintage, 1984).
4. Amory Lovins and L. Hunter: *Brittle Power* (Baltimore: Brick House Books, 1982).
5. C. G. Jung, *Man and His Symbols.* (New York: Dell, 1968).

Chapter 11

1. Eknath Easwaran, *Meditation: A Simple 8-Point Program for Transforming Spiritual Ideals Into Daily Life* (Tomales, CA: Nilgiri Press, 2001).

Chapter 12

1. Gestalt therapy, which has influenced our outlook and this book, draws several of these strands together. Fritz Perls moved from his background in theater to training as a psychoanalyst. His wife Laura, who had a background in movement and dance, trained in Gestalt theoretical and experimental psychology. The founder of Gestalt psychology, Max Wertheimer, was an accomplished philosopher who wove ideas from physics into his thinking. His students Wolfgang Kohler and Kurt Koffka studied perception and learning. Kurt Goldstein, under whom Fritz Perls served in World War I, was a Gestalt-oriented physiological and neurological psychologist. All this, as well as Wilhelm Reich's body-oriented outlook, became part of the theoretical background of Fritz and Laura. Their background in theater and movement, combined with the body-oriented psychologies of Wilhelm Reich and Kurt Goldstein and Fritz' training analyses with Reich, Karen Horney, Otto Rank and others, and later Carl Rogers' "Person Centered," fundamentally phenomenological approach that placed the client's experience at the center of the therapeutic process, laid the foundation for Gestalt Therapy. Paul Goodman and Ralph Hefferline in New York were also part of the group that developed

the approach, and coauthors with Fritz of the book *Gestalt Therapy: Excitement and Growth in the Human Personality* (New York: Dell, 1951).

2. Yoav Ben-Dov, "The Open Reading" (Israel: www.CBDTarot.com, 2013).
3. Alejandro Jodoroski and Marianne Costa. *The Way of Tarot: The Spiritual Traditions in the Cards* (Rochester, VT: Inner Traditions International, 2009).
4. Idries Shah, *The Way of the Sufi* (New York: Dutton, 1970).
5. Philip Zimbardo, *The Lucifer Effect: Understanding How Good People Turn Evil* (New York: Random House, 2008).

Epilogue
Kooch N. Daniels and Victor Daniels. *Tarot d'Amour: Find Love, Sex, and Romance in the Cards* (York Beach, ME. & Boston: Redwheel Weiser, 2003).

BIBLIOGRAPHY

Adler, Alfred. *The Individual Psychology of Alfred Adler*. Edited by H. R. and R. R. Ansbacher. NY: Harper, 1964.

_____. *Superiority and Social Interest*. NY: Viking, 1973.

Amberstone, Ruth Ann and Wald. *Tarot Tips*. St. Paul MN: Llewellen, 2003.

Amberstone, Wald and Ruth Ann. *The Secret Language of Tarot*. San Francisco: Red Wheel/Weiser, 2008.

Bandura, Albert. *Social Learning Theory*. Englewood Cliffs, NY: Prentice-Hall, 1977.

Beck, Aaron. *Cognitive Therapy and the Emotional Disorders*. NY: International Universities Press, 1976.

Ben-Dov, Yoav. *CBD Tarot de Marseille: A Faithful Reproduction of the Traditional Tarot*. (A deck and booklet). North Charleston (also Israel): Galaxy Tone Software.

Bettelheim, Bruno. *Freud and Man's Soul: An Important Re-Interpretation of Freudian Theory*. NY: Alfred A. Knopf, 1982.

Bloom, Dan and Philip Brownell, Editors. *Continuity and Change: Gestalt Therapy Now*. Newcastle Upon Tyne: Cambridge Scholars Publishing, 2011.

Bolen, Jean Shinoda. *Goddesses in Everywoman*. NY: Harper and Row, 1984.

Brownell, Philip, ed. *Handbook for Theory, Research, and Practice in Gestalt Therapy*. Newcastle Upon Tyne: Cambridge Scholars Publishing, 2008.

Bugenthal, James. *The Search for Authenticity: An Existential-Analytic Approach to Psychotherapy*. 2nd ed. NY: Holt, Rhinehart, & Winston, 1980.

Criswell, Eleanor. *How Yoga Works: An Introduction to Somatic Yoga*. Novato CA: Freeperson Press, 1989.

Criswell Eleanor. *Biofeeback and Somatics: Toward Personal Evolution*. Novato CA: Freeperson Press, 1995.

Crowley, Aleister. *The Book of Thoth* . York Beach, ME: Weiser Books, 2002.

Daniels, Kooch N. and Victor. *Tarot d'Amour: Find Love, Sex, and Romance in the Cards*. Boston and York Beach, ME: Redwheel Weiser, 2003.

Daniels, Victor and Laurence J. Horowitz. *Being and Caring: A Psychology for Living,* 2nd ed. Palo Alto: Mayfield, 1984; Long Grove, Ill: Waveland 1999.

De Beauvoir, Simone. *The Second Sex.* NY: Random House Vintage, 1961, 1989.

Dollard, John and Neal E. *Personality and Psychotherapy: An Analysis in Terms of Learning, Thinking, and Culture.* NY: McGraw Hill, 1950.

DuQuette, Lon Milo. *Understanding Aleister Crowley's Thoth Tarot.* Boston and York Beach ME, 2003.

Feder, Bud and Ruth Ronall. *A Living Legacy of Fritz and Laura Perls: Contemporary Case Studies.* Montclair, NJ: Walden Press, 1996.

Freud, Sigmund. *Collected papers, Vols.* 1-5. Edited by James Strachey. *NY: Basic Books, 1959.*

Freud, Sigmund. *The Basic Writings of Sigmund Freud.* Trans. A.A. Brill. NY: Modern Library.

Fromm, Erich. *The Art of Loving.* NY: Bantam, 1970.

Gilbert, Toni. *Gaining Archetypal Vision: A Guidebook for Using Archetypes in Personal Growth and Healing.* Atglen, PA: Schiffer Publishing, 2011.

Greer, Mary K. *Tarot for Your Self.* 2nd edition. Franklin Lakes NJ: New Page Books, 2002.

_____. *Mary K. Greer's 21 Ways to Read a Tarot Card, Kindle edition.* St. Paul, MN: Llewellen, 2011.

Jodoroski, Alejandro and Marianne Costa. *The Way of Tarot: The Spiritual Teacher in the Cards.* Translated by Jon E. Graham. RochesterVT: Destiny Books, 2009.

Horney, Karen. *Neurosis and Human Growth.* NY: Norton, 1950.

Jourard, Sidney. *Disclosing Man to Himself.* Princeton NJ: Van Nostrand, 1968.

Jung, Carl G. *The Collected Works of Carl G. Jung. 2nd ed., Bollingen Series 20.* Princeton, NJ: Princeton University Press, 1960–72.

Jung, Carl G. *Sychronicity: An Acausal Connecting Principle.* Trans. R. F. Hull. Ed. G. Adler. Princeton University Press, 1973.

Kaplan, Stuart R. *Encyclopedia of Tarot, Vol. 1.* NY: U.S. Games Systems, 1985.

Keleman, Stanley. *Your Body Speaks Its Mind.* NY: Pocket Books, 1976.

Kelley, Harold H. *Personal Relationships: Their Structures and Processess.* Hillsdale NJ: Laurence Erlbaum, 1979.

Kierkegaard, Soren and Howard V. Hong. *The Essential Kierkegaard.* Princeton, NJ: Princeton University Press, 1978.

Lewin, Kurt. *Field Theory in Social Science*. Ed. by Dorwin Cartwright. NY: Harper & Row, 1951.

Lovins, Amory & Hunter. *Brittle Power: Energy Strategy for National Security*. Brick House Publishing Company,1982.

Maslow, Abraham. *Religions, Values, and Peak Experiences*. NY: Penguin, 1976.

May, Rollo. *The Courage to Create*. NY: Bantam, 1976.

Merleau-Ponty, Maurice. *The Primacy of Perception*. Edited by James M. Edie. Evanston IL: Northwestern University Press, 1964.

Murray, Henry. *Endeavors in Psychology*. Ed. by Edwin S. Schneidman. NY: Harper & Row, 1981.

Naranjo, Claudio. *Gestalt Therapy: The Attitude and Practice of an Atheoretical Experientialism*. Nevada City CA: Gateways/IDHHB, 1993.

Nichols, Sallie. *Jung and Tarot: An Archetypal Journey*. York Beach ME: Weiser Books, 1991.

Ouspensky, P. D. *The Symbolism of the Tarot: Philosophy of Occultism in Pictures*. Trans A. L. Pogossky. NY: Dover Publications, 1976.

Palladini, David and Anastasia Haysler. *Painting the Soul: The Tarot Art of David Palladini*. San Francisco CA: Black Swan Press, 2013.

Perls, Frederick S. [Fritz] *Ego, Hunger, and Aggression: The Beginning of Gestalt Therapy*. NY: Random House, 1947.

_____. *Gestalt Therapy Verbatim*. NY: The Gestalt Journal Press, 1988.

_____. *In and Out of the Garbage Pail*. Highland NY: The Gestalt Journal Press, 1988.

_____Ralph F. Hefferline, and Paul Goodman. *Gestalt Therapy: Excitement and Growth in the Human Personality*. NY: Dell, 1965.

Pelletier, Kenneth R. *Mind as Healer, Mind as Slayer: A Holistic Approach to Preventing Stress Disorders*. NY: Dell, 1977.

Philippson, Peter. *Self in Relation*. Highland NY: Gestalt Journal Press, 2001.

Place, Robert. *Alchemy and the Tarot*. Saugerties NY: Hermes Publications, 2011.

Pollack, Rachel. *Seventy-Eight Degrees of Wisdom: A Book of Tarot*. – Revised edition. ME: Weiser Books, 2007.

Polster, Erving. *Every Person's Life is Worth a Novel*. NY: Norton, 1987.

Polster, Erving and Miriam. *From the Radical Center: The Heart of Gestalt*. Gestalt Institute, 2000

Rogers, Carl. *On Becoming a Person: A Therapist's View of Psychotherapy*. Boston MA: Houghton Mifflin, 1961.

_____. *On Personal Power*. NY: Delacorte, 1977.

Rosengarten, Art. *Tarot and Psychology: Spectrums of Possibility*. St. Paul MN: Paragon House, 2000.

Sartre, Jean Paul. *Essays in Existentialism*. Seacaucus NJ: Citadel Press, 1967.

Schneider, Kirk J. and Rollo May. *The Psychology of Existence: An Integrative, Clinical Perspective*. NY: McGraw Hill, 1995.

Seligman, Martin E.P. *Helplessness: On Depression. Development, and Death*. San Francisco: Freeman, 1977.

Siegel, Daniel. *Mindsight: The New Science of Personal Transformation*. NY: Bantam, 2010.

_____. *The Mindful Therapist: A Clinician's Guide to Mindsight and Neural Integration*. NY: Norton, 2010

Shah, Idries. *The Way of the Sufi*. NY: Dutton, 1970.

Skinner, B. F. *Science and Human Behavior*. NY: Macmillan, 1053

Teachworth, Ann. *Why We Pick the Mates We Do*. Metarie/New Orleans: Gestalt Institute Press, 2002

Tolman, Edward Chace. *Purposive Behavior in Animals and Men*. Berkeley: University of California Press, 1949.

Wanless, James. *Voyager Tarot: Way of the Great Oracle*. Carmel CA: Merrill West Publishing, 1989.

Wertheimer, Max. *Productive Thinking*. Westport CT: Greenwood Press, 1978.

Woldt, Ansel L. and Sarah M. Toman. *Gestalt Therapy: History, Theory and Practice*. Thousand Oaks CA: SAGE Publications, 2005.

Wheeler, Gordon and Stephanie Backman, eds. *On Intimate Ground: A Gestalt Approach to Working With Couples*. San Francisco CA: Jossey Bass, 1994.

Wynne, Katrina. *An Introduction to Tarot Counseling: The High Art of Reading*. Yachats OR: Sacred Rose Publishing, 2012.

Yalom, Irvin. *The Gift of Therapy: An Open Letter to a New Generation of Therapists and Their Patients*. NY: HarperCollins 2013.

Yontef, Gary M. *Awareness Dialogue & Process: Essays on Gestalt Therapy*. Highland, NY: The Gestalt Journal Press, 1993.

Zimbardo, Philip. *The Lucifer Effect: Understanding How Good People Turn Evil*. NY: Random House, 2007.

INDEX

Jung, Carl, 21–2, 23, 34, 43, 51, 99, 151, 153, 183, 196–7, 252, 255–6, 259, 260.
Jung, C.G. (See *Jung, Carl*).

K
Kahn, Aunia, 9, 11, 12.
Kalff, Dora, 22.
Kelley, Harold H., 207.
kindness, 146, 182, 186–7, 191, 203, 214
Kozmic Koffee with Kooch, 9. (also spelled Kosmic. . .)

L
Lenormand, 13.
life-space, 51–53, 138, 160, 161
listen, listening, 28, 45, 60, 62, 85, 109, 110, 113, 125, 139, 142, 150, 158, 173, 181, 186, 187, 190, 192, 197, 199, 206–7, 209, 219, 224, 231, 237, 241, 248.
love or lover(s), 3, 19–20, 33–4, 40, 42, 66–70, 107, 114, 119, 134, 140–43, 146, 153, 179, 182, 184–5, 188–190, 191–2, 197–8, 199, 203, 211, 214–15, 220, 223, 225, 229–31, 241, 243–4, 247, 249, 250.
Lovers, the, a card in the Major Arcana, 140–43, 188, 230, 253.
Lowenfeld, Margaret, 22.

M
Maffei, Raphaelis, 20.
Marseilles Deck, 12, 20, 32.
McClure, Chris, 8.
meanings of cards, traditional and personal, 14–17, 26–7, 31, 32–4, 36–7, 46, 49–50, 53–5, 71, 75–6, 112, 116, 139, 140–1, 157, 159, 166, 176, 178–208, 210–11, 218, 241.
movies, 52.
movies, mental- or mind-, 22, 25, 69, 75.
Mexican Gestalt Association, 9.
Michelino Deck, 20.
Milan, Italy, 20.
momentum, 149.
mindfulness (See also *attention, awareness, witness consciousness*) , 146, 167, 197.

Q

Queen of Swords, 3, 20, 124, 247.

querent, 25, 27, 33, 41, 43, 46–50, 55–56, 58, 60, 64, 68, 76, 79, 87–8, 10 9, 113, 118, 123–4, 134, 145, 156, 157–60, 171, 173, 197, 215–16, 244, 250, 252.

questions, 19, 51, 60, 64, 69, 82–3, 89, 102, 106, 107, 111–12, 117, 123–5, 141, 147, 154–8, 161–4, 196, 216, 250, 252.

R

reaction(s), 26–7, 32–4, 38–40, 43, 46–7, 51, 55, 58, 60, 72, 88, 113, 117, 139, 141, 157–8, 161, 168–9, 195, 223, 236, 251, 255.

readers and reading (See also *divinatory readings and methods*), 2, 6, 8, 10, 13–15, 19 25–, 22–28, 30, 33, 50, 59, 62, 106, 123, 138, 147, 157, 170.

Reader's Studio Tarot Conference, 2, 8, 14, 26.

Reich, Wilhelm, 22, 199, 256.

representational methods, 7, 15–17, 27, 32, 36, 40, 42, 50, 52, 54–56, 60, 64, 73, 104, 107–118, 120–134, 140–141, 163–5, 219, 251.

resolve (See *determination,* also *perseverance*).

respect, 111, 188, 190, 206, 212, 214, 224, 228, 247.

responsible, responsibility, 6, 142, 186, 188, 192–3. 216, 234–5, 242.

Rider Waite Coleman Smith Deck, 16, 33.

Rivera, J.R. 9, 11, 12.

Rogers, Carl, 22–3, 146, 159, 206, 256, 261.

Rorschach, Hermann, 24.

Rorschach inkblot test, 24.

Roseberry, Dinah, 9.

Rosengarten, Art, 9, 99, 255, 261.

S

sand tray, 22–4, 87.

sand play therapy, 22–4.

Schick, Major Tom, 9, 12.

Schiffer, Pete, 12.

Schiffer Publishing, 6, 8, 9, 12, 16.

self-deception, 183, 196.

self-determination (See *authenticity*).

self-righteousness (See also *self–deception*), 187.

Seilonen, Beth, 9, 11, 12.

ABOUT THE AUTHORS

Victor Daniels, who received his PhD from UCLA, is Emeritus Professor of Psychology at Sonoma State University, where he taught for forty-one years and served as department chair. He has been using the Tarot as a tool for psychological insight and personal growth for many years. Having taught Gestalt therapy and done many hundreds of Tarot readings, it seemed natural for him to combine his Gestalt training techniques with the symbolic playing field of the Tarot. Visit his websites at:

www.sonoma.edu/users/d/daniels
and consciousnessandculture.com.

Kooch N. Daniels is a life-long intuitive who has given many thousands of Tarot readings. She enjoys the study of mystical spirituality, oracular traditions, and transpersonal psychology. Sole author of several books, she also enjoys co-writing with her husband, Victor. Together they have written *Tarot d'Amour: Find Love, Sex, and Romance in the Cards*, and *Matrix Meditations: . . . For Developing The Mind-Heart Connection*.

Visit her website at: www.cybermystic.com.

OTHER SCHIFFER BOOKS
ON RELATED SUBJECTS

TAROT AND THE CHAKRAS
Opening New Dimensions to Healers
Miriam Jacobs
ISBN: 978-0-7643-4663-7

TAROT IN REVERSE
Making Sense of the Upside Down Cards in a Tarot Spread
Janet Boyer
ISBN: 978-0-7643-4101-4

TAROT SPREADS AND LAYOUTS
A User's Manual For Beginning and Intermediate Readers
Jeanne Fiorini
ISBN: 978-0-7643-3629-4

TAROT, RITUALS & YOU
The Power of Tarot Combined with the Power of Ritual
Bonnie Cehovet
ISBN: 978-0-7643-4318-6